GOD
ALWAYS
GIVES YOU
WHAT YOU
WANT

MICHAEL YANCEY, JR.

Written by Michael Yancey, Jr.

Published by Yancey Publishing,
a ministry of Michael Yancey, Jr.

Edited by: Kathy Wright

Illustrations, Interior Page Design and Layout, and
Cover Design and Layout by Robert Scott/Clear Graphics

GOD ALWAYS GIVES YOU WHAT YOU WANT

"I have made every effort to acknowledge and document any outside sources. If there is found any material in this book which has not been properly accredited to the source, please accept this disclaimer as proof of my desire and purpose."-Michael Yancey, Jr.

www.facebook.com/GodAlwaysGivesYouWhatYouWant

Menu

Foreword

Due to the honest opinion of a close friend and professional in many respects, Lyndell Durr, I have stepped up to bat as an author.

The love and assistance of many more has also made this project possible.

Kathy Wright, my editor, has been a tremendous help in cooperating with me to preserve my style and thought-flow while offering the necessary corrections. She has done a fantastic job.

Robert Scott has worked tirelessly and with true creativity as an artist and graphics designer to make me happy with the finished product: it has not been easy!

My wife, Regina, has proof-read every bit of this material, giving sharp observations and gentle corrections.

My cheer-leading team, the rest of the brood, has encouraged me greatly. Thank you, Michael, David, Joshua, and Brooklynn, Mom and Dad, Regina and Alina, my sisters, for your love and support. You have been the fire in the space-ship to get us air-borne and to the destination!

Last of all, to the audience, thank you for your vote of confidence, or just plain curiosity, for purchasing this book.

Michael Yancey, Jr.

Introduction
"just what is this book about?"

This book is a ***collection of reflections*** from a traveler on the road of life, where eternity resides in each step toward the City of God.

It is a ***collection of visions*** this traveler has seen from the hard-earned mountaintop, visions captured as he stood looking far down the path he had just climbed, finally seeing things from a better perspective.

And it is a ***collection of mysteries*** of the Christian journey which the traveler has attempted to unravel: the stinging, probing questions that pierce the soul, scratch the surface of life, and threaten to debilitate the pilgrim. Questions that stick like cockle-burrs in our minds and spirits and cannot be plucked free even in our old age.

This book will not tell you how to avoid the challenges of the journey, but it may provide you with a few potions, or antidotes, for the pricks and scratches you yourself have endured along the way.

It may give you a helping hand up if you have fallen, or point you in the right direction at a crossroads.

It may wipe a sleeve across the skylight of your soul so that you can see God more clearly, or it may just be a drink of water.

> "It is a collection of visions this traveler has seen from the hard-earned mountaintop, visions captured as he stood looking far down the path he had just climbed, finally seeing things from a better perspective."

Whatever it does for you, if it helps you on your journey, it was well worth my effort in keeping this Journal.

Hope to see you in Heaven!

Michael Yancey, Jr.

God Always Gives You What you Want
God's secret design for your life

Not many people believe this, not even in Christian circles.

We can quite quickly come up with a long list of things we wished for, asked for, hoped for... but never got and never will get!

We can also very quickly come up with a list of relationships, jobs, and unhappy events in our lives that seem to argue strongly against this thought.

But before you close this book, please hear me out. I will start by telling you a story.

"I have watched as lives have spun out of control and people who many years before had such promise somehow end up with problems that handicap or cripple them in their striving for success in life."

Many years ago I attended a Bible college to earn my theology degree. While there I met a young lady infused with a quiet and steady spirit, the daughter of a very godly pastor. My first recollection of her was her crying in the dark in the administration building one

"He then showed me in all those faces very special people put there by Himself to hone and further develop the very desire of my heart."

night, all by herself. I did not know this girl, but I tried to console her by listening to her story. Her dad was in such bad shape physically that he was having to resign his pastorate and had a very small chance of surviving due to a heart condition. Thankfully, today God has turned his condition around and he has lived twenty years when he was not supposed to last five.

This conversation in the administration building was the beginning of a relationship that grew over a period of two years. We did not officially date during this time, but we recognized that some kind of special feeling was growing between us. To help us along our romantic journey, the registrar and a teacher in the college encouraged us, prayed for us, and thought we were "meant for each other." One night (on my first official date with her) I asked this girl to marry me. I was certain!

One might say, "The rest is history"; but that seems too trite to me. I have seen many marriages fail in the last twenty-plus years of ours. I have seen homes break up, children suffer, ministries crash and burn. I have watched as lives have spun out of control and people who many years before had such promise somehow end up with problems that handicap or cripple them in their striving for success in life.

But back to the story...

Recently I began thinking of that very precious, elderly lady who had taught me in Bible college and done her best to get Regina and me together. Now she is retired, a widow. I called her and she was as sweet as ever. As we visited, she asked me if I would like some pictures that she had of me and my wife when we were dating. "You can show them to your children and prove to them that you were romantic at one time," she teased.

I replied that I would love to have them. Weeks later the package arrived; and while I held each one, memories flooded my mind of those young days.

"They had wanted something so badly at some point that they had wanted it more than God's will. And they got what they wanted."

The next morning I went on one of my devotional strolls in the cold winter hours. Picking my way through some icy spots on a snow-laden hill, I reflected upon those pictures Sister Rosa had sent me.

I began to thank God for His gift to me through my wife and for her blessing and influence throughout my life. As a college student, I'd had no idea what a perfect match this person made by God would be for me.

God then revealed something I had never seen before. He showed me how that, though ignorant of the years ahead and all that life would bring us, I had been given a very special gift. Not just any girl, but a very special someone who would be used of Him to change me for the good and to encourage the instincts of my heart for Himself.

"God always gives you what you want, whether good or bad."

He then took me down the trail of life and showed me different ones who had come and gone: faces and friendships which had budded and bloomed and then faded away into the winter of memories. He then showed me in all those faces very special people put there by Himself to hone and further develop the very desire of my heart. He helped me to reflect on some of the most painful circumstances in my life and showed me how even those were allowed by Him to lead me on my very special journey. He then showed me that all through life I had been given what I really wanted all along. He had *personally* handpicked situations and people to serve the great purpose of my soul. Regardless of what appeared on the outside, God had known all along the deepest desires of my heart and had rewarded me accordingly.

This stirred my heart deeply. Then I began to muse on others who were reaping the results of what they had wanted… those crashed marriages, those broken homes, those handicapped ministries. They had wanted something so badly at some point that they had wanted it more than God's will. And they got what they wanted.

I began to pray for my children and their desires. Then the Lord seemed to say, "Mike, I will give to your children exactly what they ultimately want. I will be faithful and fair to their hearts as I was to yours."

From this private interview came this thought: *God always gives you what you want, whether good or bad.*

We as Christians quote verses like "Ask and it will be given to you; seek and you will find; knock and the door will be opened to you. Everyone who asks receives; the one who seeks finds; and to the one who knocks, the door will be opened" (Matthew 7:7). Then we quickly add the disclaimer: "Delight yourself in the LORD, and he will give you the desires of your heart" (Psalm 37:4). But the real truth is, God will let every man, woman, and child have his or her way. He gives us the choice

"But you can know this: If you want it, God will give you His perfect will that will make you happy beyond comprehension as you walk the trail of life."

between His perfect will for our lives or our own way. And once we make that choice, He gives us the deepest desires of our heart, regardless of our devotion to Him. *God always gives you what you want!*

I hope the chapters in this book will stir your soul and help you to strive with all your heart to seek the best God has to give you.

As with my wife, you sometimes just don't know until later how precious the gift is that God has wrapped in a pretty bow and handed to you. As with hard circumstances, you sometimes cannot judge a gift by its brown wrapping paper. But you can know this: If you want it, God will give you His perfect will that will make you happy beyond comprehension as you walk the trail of life.

Horace Bushnell, the great Yale preacher from the nineteenth century said, *"The only men who are confident in their purpose of life, content, are those who have surrendered completely, who walk everyday in His light, who thrill at His revealed next step."*

Buckle your seatbelt and enjoy the ride!

The Scarlet Cord
a wonderful start

Joshua 2:21: "After she sent the spies on their way she tied the red cord in the window."

Not everybody is born with a spiritual silver spoon in his or her mouth. Many people have no memories of church attendance and godly parents or grandparents. The story you are about to read tells you that no matter where you started in life, God has a bright future for you. Your path through life can lead, as Proverbs says, to an ever- brightening day (4:18).

> "Not everybody is born with a spiritual silver spoon in his or her mouth."

(The following rendition of this Bible story has been greatly expanded according to the imagination of one humble writer.)

Madame Rahab, proprietor of a local brothel, drew back the curtains of her sleepy establishment to allow the morning sun's harsh rays to probe and warm the cool darkness of the night. She vigorously popped the porch rug and whisked away the dried dirt tracks of the steady stream of visitors from the night before. With a slap, the morning edition of the *Jericho Times* landed at her feet, shouting "Israel is at our border and threatens to invade our land!" As she clutched the paper, dark clouds of worry crept over her countenance as she involuntarily gazed toward the distant Jordan River. She had heard of this motley gathering of redeemed slaves. Over one hundred years ago the Pharaoh of distant Egypt had ordered their genocide by two primeval types of abortion. Both had failed. Instead of extinction, they had only swelled in numbers and were now ready to invade her own land.

"*. . . no matter where you started in life, God has a bright future for you.*"

"*In Rahab's house a trunk full of old yellowed newspapers chronicled their story.*"

In Rahab's house a trunk full of old yellowed newspapers chronicled their story. One clipping started with Israel's local folk-hero-turned-political-criminal named Moses. He had coined the undying phrase, "Let my people GO," which had become a rallying cry for this multitude. The Pharaoh had laughingly refused this demand and increased their work load for the trouble!

But for *his* impudence, according to the *Egyptian Weekly* and *Jericho Times*, Moses' wand had produced plagues that ruined their drinking water, filled their streets with frogs, and killed their cattle with hail. After each blow, Moses would show up again with the same ridiculous request. "Why didn't they just kill the rabble-rouser and be done with it?" everyone had wondered.

She then remembered another yellowed copy which climaxed this awful uprising. It had announced, "Egypt has fallen and Israel is on the move!" This one had a sketch of great Red Sea waves crashing in upon the Egyptian armies underneath the wand of Moses.

Then all news of Israel had gone virtually silent for forty years. Occasionally, she would hear of their whereabouts in her establishment, where gossip flowed as freely as money, whiskey, and morals in the dimly lit, smoke-filled rooms: stories of manna from heaven, water from a rock, a strange cloud by day and a pillar of fire, and shoes and clothes that never wore out.

But this morning, there was no doubt where they were: at Canaan's borders with blood in their eyes.

Jericho quickly became a madhouse of people scurrying around, stocking up on supplies. Young soldiers flexed their muscles, threatening violence to the enemy who breached their borders. The mayor of the town consulted with his engineers about the integrity of the walls and gates in case of a siege. Occult priests of local demons offered extra sacrifices for the safety of the city. Many laughed nervously about the silliness of these foreigners trying to take their land and city.

> "While all sand-bagged their confidence against the feared intrusion, Rahab had chosen a different response."

While all sand-bagged their confidence against the feared intrusion, Rahab had chosen a different response. Wistfully folding the newspaper, she re-entered her place of business and scanned the faces of her sleepy workforce: women whose eyes were clouded with wariness, worthlessness, and a sickly weariness. Suddenly Rahab *herself* was tired: tired of her life, tired of the struggle, tired of the type of people with whom she associated. And she was truly afraid.

She went about her business through the next few nights preoccupied, like everyone else, with the disturbing news. Then one night her ladies approached her with a strange request from two visitors. They needed to be hidden. Taking them to her own private room for an interview, she grew increasingly alarmed as she realized that these men were spies from the feared Israeli camp. Definitely different, their gaze was direct, their language clean, and their questions probing. They had no interest in her beverages or her line up of women. She discreetly fulfilled their request for anonymity and invisibility and returned to her own room.

> "Suddenly, taking her night candle, she resolutely exited her room and mounted a flight of stairs."

This was an unexpected opportunity. She could simply turn them in to the authorities to be amply rewarded and praised. Or, she could take a different path. What would she do? She nervously paced the floor of her room, searching for the answer deep in her soul.

Suddenly, taking her night candle, she resolutely exited her room and mounted a flight of stairs. She tapped lightly on their door. Granted entrance, she sat upon the side of their bed and said, "I know who you are!" And then she expressed her fear.

But this wasn't just any kind of fear. It was special. Heaven-sent. You see, God had promised Abraham that He would drive out the inhabitants of Canaan when their cup of iniquity was full. Then He had promised Joshua that He would send *His* fear before the Israelites into the hearts of the Canaanites to break the back of their resistance. Thus, this was not human fear, but fear of a great God whose armies of heaven were advancing through the armies of Joshua. She confessed, "The terror of you has fallen on us!" (Joshua 2:9-11). She saw it in the eyes and heard it in the voices of her neighbors and leaders. She recognized it in her own bosom. But unlike her own people, she chose to face her fear in a way that changed her future. Instead of bracing herself against it, she folded and confessed, throwing herself upon their mercy.

What a beautiful thing to do: to throw yourself upon the mercy of God!

"Please," she said, "take me with you and save my family, for we know God has delivered this country into your hands!"

Her heart-felt plea touched the spies. They gave her one duty to perform to ensure her own salvation and that of her family: "When we are gone, let down this scarlet cord as a signal of your identity and location."

> "Under the cover of darkness she let them down over the wall; and when the morning sun lit the sky, from a window sill dangled a red rope, lazily bouncing in the morning breeze."

Under the cover of darkness she let them down over the wall; and when the morning sun lit the sky, from a window sill dangled a red rope, lazily bouncing in the morning breeze.

Off in the distance the Jordan River opened its arms to welcome the new army. The tramp of the soldiers sent tremors through the ground. Citizens of Jericho peered over their walls, nervously and smugly observing this strange military sporting no catapults, battering rams, or wall-scaling ladders. The silence of fear and awe gripped the land. Only the tramping of feet and the pealing of trumpet

notes punctured the stillness. Round and round Israel
marched, day after day, without a word. On the seventh
day, suddenly the marching stopped.
Priests pressed long trumpets to their
lips and blew hard and long.

"Did you notice that thousands of years later, Scripture still called her a harlot? Why?"

A war cry erupted from the
soldiers like the roar of a furnace.
Reverberating sound waves magnified
by a heavenly megaphone smacked against the great
walls of the city; and, like a boy swiping an army of
plastic men, the walls imploded in geysers of dust.

A stunned silence followed the
concussion as Jericho found itself
face to face with the Israeli army, the
army the Pharaoh of distant Egypt had
followed to his death in the Red Sea.

". . . there is one common denominator among the untold numbers that walk the streets of gold in Heaven: their robes are washed in the blood of the Lamb."

With a cry Israel rushed in over
the rubble and crushed the resistance
completely.

When the sound of war had died
away, among the rubble and carnage
stood one lonely part of Jericho's
famed wall, now trimmed in jagged edges where the
great downed wall had been ripped from it on either side.
And a red cord bounced along in the hot breeze outside
one lonely window.

Suddenly Rahab heard a gentle knock on her door,
and a familiar voice called her name. With scarves

wrapped around their faces, Rahab and her family were escorted safely to the outskirts of the city.

"You can read about her, but not in some old newspaper from an old trunk. You can go right to the Bible to see her story!"

Now I ask you a question: Why was she saved? What about Rahab kept her from the fate of her fathers and countrymen?

I would like to answer that it was not because of her profession! She was a "soiled dove." It was her faith in Israel's God and her willingness to throw herself upon His mercy.

Hebrews 11:31 says, "By faith *the harlot Rahab* perished not with them that believed not, when she had received the spies with peace." Regardless of her start, God saw her heart and extended a hand of mercy by sending the spies to her place.

"And it all started with a lonely, swinging rope of scarlet, dangling in the breeze, testimony to a heart who wanted another chance, a different life, and a better God."

Did you notice that thousands of years later, Scripture still called her a harlot? Why? This name is not meant to embarrass her, but rather to be a testimony to the tremendous change God can effect in the darkest of hearts. She did not start out as a lily white flower, but rather as a soiled dove. Hers is not the only story like this. In Mark 14 we read that Christ visited the home of Simon the Leper. This did not mean he was still a leper, but that he was a leper *before* Christ met him. Matthew has been called the tax collector for thousands of years--but only to refer to what he was *before* he encountered Jesus. Mary Magdalene is referred to as the "one out of whom He had cast seven devils," but her past was referenced only to identify her as one whom the Master had delivered.

Dottie Rambo wrote a fitting song:

> I boast not of works or tell of good deeds,
> For naught have I done to merit His grace.
> All glory and praise shall rest upon Him,
> So willing to die in my place.
>
> My trophies and crowns, my robe
> stained with sin –
> 'Twas all that I had to lay at His feet.
> Unworthy to eat from the table of Life
> 'Til Love made provision for me.
>
> I will glory in the cross, in the cross,
> Lest His suffering all be in vain.
> I will weep no more for the cross that He bore;
> I will glory in the cross.

I might remind you that there is one common denominator among the untold numbers that walk the streets of gold in Heaven: their robes are *washed* in the blood of the Lamb. They didn't get there without a bath – a heavenly bath, that is.

Rahab's story teaches us that we don't have to approach God with "doctored up" character resumes, immigration papers, and spiritual passports. He knows who we are. All we have to do is hang the scarlet cord out our window. We need mercy, and there is a God who has plenty!

Was it not on the cross that a sinner, heaving his last ragged gasps of life-giving air, met a Stranger who did not belong on a cross? This thief's spirit was facing the door of death when he glanced desperately into the face of this Stranger who faced the same door. Afraid to cross that threshold and face the eternal punishment for what he was, he asked if the Stranger would take his arm and help him through. On his worst day, Christ took the arm of the thief and ushered him into the very presence of a loving God. This desperate man didn't ask for anything but mercy. He simply let down a scarlet cord over the sill of his window, and forever his destiny was changed.

Yours can be too!

Because of Rahab's scarlet cord, a couple things happened.

Her family was saved. Your family will forever thank you if you make the right choice to let down the cord.

Her name and choice became immortal instead of being buried in the rubble of history. Huddled with her family on the outskirts of town, she watched the flames leap high and consume the scene of her past life. Then she turned, hand in hand with Salmon, one of those very spies she had hidden, and started a new life.

You can read about her, but not in some old newspaper from an old trunk. You can go right to the Bible to see her story! Through her marriage, she became the great-great grandmother of King David, part of the Messianic line. Besides Sarah, she is the only woman mentioned in the great cloud of witnesses for their faith, right beside Enoch, Moses, Abraham, Joseph, Noah, and David.

And it all started with a lonely, swinging rope of scarlet, dangling in the breeze, testimony to a heart who wanted another chance, a different life, and a better God.

What about you? Do you stand with the multitude or with Rahab? Are the gates of your heart shut hard against the advance of God and His army, or is the cord of faith dangling from the window of your heart?

Madame Rahab, I plan to meet you in heaven. I shall be glad to tell you that your story inspired me and millions of others. Thank you for hanging a scarlet rope out the window sill of your heart!

Michael Yancey, Jr.

An Unfriendly Wasp
beware of dark desires

A long time ago, a mother sat in the front seat of a carriage while her spoiled child sat in the back seat with the family's maid. Along the journey the little child began screaming for something (as we see children act in the stores with their parents today). The mother, without looking back, asked the maid why the child was crying, as if to say the disruption was the maid's fault.

"... the nurse, with a sense of poetic justice, allowed the child to reach out and grab what he had been unsuccessfully trying to get."

"I won't give him what he want," the maid replied.

"Well, why don't you give him what he wants?!" the

mother said impatiently, while thinking *That will surely shut up the kid.*

So the nurse, with a sense of poetic justice, allowed the child to reach out and grab what he had been unsuccessfully trying to get. To the mother's surprise, the child screamed even more. Frustrated, the mother, without looking around, cried, "What is the matter with him now?!"

"He got what he wanted," the maid explained.

"Desires can be dangerous things, without our even knowing it."

What he had wanted was a wasp crawling along the window, minding its own business.

Let's talk about what you want.

Desires can be dangerous things, without our even knowing it. Solomon shares a sage quote: "*The prosperity of fools shall destroy them*" (Proverbs 1:32). Believing we are successful without God's blessing is very dangerous. Spurgeon, the great English Baptist preacher was approached one night by a stranger after he had preached on the lost lamb. The man spoke to him.

"Dr. Spurgeon, I wish I had known you were going to preach on that story. I could have given you a wonderful illustration. I'm a hunter, and not long ago I went with a guide to hunt in the mountains of Scotland. We stopped for lunch on a little plateau that was surrounded by mountains and high grassy plains. I picked up my binoculars and searched the mountains around us. On one of them there was a sheep far below the top of another high plateau. I handed my binoculars to my guide and said, 'Look. How will he ever get back?'

"The wise old guide, who had spent his life in those mountains, said sadly, 'He can't get back alone. He has left the flock and, unnoticed by the shepherd, has jumped down to a grassy ledge. After he ate the grass on that ledge, he jumped down to the one below. Unless the shepherd finds him quickly and helps him back he is lost, for the eagles have already seen him and are circling above him. One of them will come down screaming and flapping his wings, and the scared sheep will fall off the ledge.'

"We watched for a half hour and then the prophecy of my guide came true. It was a heartbreaking scene."

Men who believe they are successful apart from God's will are truly feeding their own ultimate failure. Like the ignorant sheep, they are going off on their own; and the eagles are circling.

This brings to mind a story of the Israelites in the wilderness, where they were successful in getting what they wanted.

Psalm 106:13-15 says:

> They quickly forgot his works (his mercy and love);
> They waited not for his counsel (they grew impatient with Him);

They lusted exceedingly in the wilderness (became very determined to have what they wanted).

He gave them their request; but sent leanness into their soul

(a wasting disease that took the body they were trying to satisfy).

The Israelites found themselves in a jam, or so they thought. There was a mixed multitude that set up a cry about the menu. They were tired of traveling food and wanted a real meal. They remembered sitting down to a table full of food prepared in ovens and seasoned with all the Egyptian spices. They remembered sitting back and patting their stomachs and licking their lips after a good meal. But now they were getting MREs for every meal, and they were tired of them. This dark dissatisfaction began to spread from man to man, woman to woman, and house to house. They began to focus on their "predicament" so much that they went from wearing long faces to feeling sorry for themselves to sniffling. Then they progressed to the whole camp sitting in their tent doors and setting up a wail that sounded like a calf bawling when it had lost its mother. The cry reached the ears of God and Moses. And they weren't happy.

"The Israelites found themselves in a jam, or so they thought."

"This dark dissatisfaction began to spread from man to man, woman to woman, and house to house."

God gave them something different. He gave them what they wanted. He sent so many quails in from the sea that they covered the land three feet deep and two days' journey wide. Oh, they gathered and gorged, which is usually what initially happens to someone who has gotten his way if God doesn't stop him. But while the flesh was still in their teeth, the anger of the Lord struck them with a plague that killed those who had lusted and caused a problem. They dug graves for those with the flesh still in their teeth. The place was called "Kibbroth- Hattavah" or "the grave of longing." I have seen many buried in that cemetery. They got something in their head, wanted it so badly that God let them have it, and then paid the price for their wrong desire.

> "God gave them something different. He gave them what they wanted."

Choosing what you naturally want versus choosing God's way is a very serious matter. It will become a crisis, a critical fork in the road. It is not something which should be treated lightly.

I have always liked a good steak and am somewhat picky about where I order one. For years, up until recently, I had always chosen Texas Roadhouse because they consistently seasoned and cooked their steaks to my liking. I still like them, but I am growing a little older and their noise is a little too much for me most of the time. One day a dear family in our church invited us to go eat with

> "The place was called 'Kibbroth – Hattavah' or 'the grave of longing.'"

them at a restaurant in Tulsa to which I had never been: Longhorn Steakhouse. We had a wonderful meal. The steak was delicious, the service great. The atmosphere was calmer than that of Texas Roadhouse. Suddenly I leaned back with a satisfied smile and full tummy and thought to myself, *Texas Roadhouse, you are fired!* Now what I did that day was only a matter of taste and personal preference. It was not a momentous, life-changing event. It did not change my spiritual destiny. It was only a choice between two steakhouses.

"We have simply made a decision to eat at Longhorn Steakhouse instead of Texas Roadhouse. Have a nice life."

When I think about that transaction, I am reminded of a story on a spiritual level which happened in my local church. When I went to pastor my current church, there had been an exodus of many families over the preceding years. A particular family had been brought to my attention as a possible prospect for returning to our church. They had moved away for a few years and were thinking of returning to Tulsa. We were excited.

"Suddenly, that bowl of beans became a pricey commodity."

I made some phone calls and thought there might be a good chance of their coming back to the church. Then one day I made a call that deflated my optimistic balloon. His reply went something like this:

"We are going to find a church in the area where we are moving, north of Tulsa. We don't know if there are any, but we want to find somewhere close to us where we can get our son back to attending."

It sounded like an admirable cause. But it also smacked of something else. It seemed to say, "There are all kinds of churches out there that preach what we want to hear. We are sure we will be satisfied with something up there as much as we would be at your church. We have simply made a decision to eat at Longhorn Steakhouse instead of Texas Roadhouse. Have a nice life." Selecting a church seemed like no big deal; just a little different seasoning, a shorter drive, and a slightly different atmosphere to them, along with an "admirable reason." I have seen many make those kinds of momentous decisions very lightly.

This reminds me of the story of Esau selling his birthright for a bowl of beans. It was actually a serious transaction with lasting consequences. Esau and Jacob were two brothers who had been competing since their birth. Jacob's name even meant "heel-grasper" because when he was born, he had hold of Esau's heel. His action was symbolic, for he consistently fought with Esau over dominance and privilege. The competition even played silently on the parental level, for scripture says Isaac favored Esau while Rebekah preferred Jacob.

"Basically, the birthright and blessing were two parts of the same thing. The two could not be separated, but this did not stop Esau from trying!"

There are two moving scenes that capture the great struggle between these brothers. The first is when Esau was coming home empty-handed from the chase. With nothing to cook, he happened to stop by Jacob's house on the way home. Jacob was cooking something that smelled delicious. Esau leaned upon his brother's good will and asked for some of that "red stuff." He didn't even know enough about culinary excellence to know its name…just "red stuff." Jacob readily agreed to ladle a healthy portion out for him, but contingent upon a strange request:

"Trade your birthright for it."

"It is true that God says, "You can have what you want." But, like the little guy in the carriage, will you be happy with what you get? "

Suddenly, that bowl of beans became a pricey commodity. I am sure Esau started at the request, but suddenly he capitulated.

"You can have it."

He was not one to be denied what he wanted, when he wanted it, regardless of some "spiritual" birthright handed down from Abraham to Isaac and now to Esau. Recklessly, he invented a "reason" for selling it. Jacob had him over a barrel. What good was a birthright going to do him if he was dead from starvation? So Jacob dished up the beans and we read these revealing words: "Esau sat down and ate and drank and rose up and went his way." That is almost a summary of Esau's life. He thought that was the end of the story. But it wasn't.

The day came when his father was fearing death. In a quivering voice he asked Esau to fetch him a fresh kill and to prepare it by the family's favorite recipe in return for the blessing of the firstborn being conferred upon him. This was a "private conversation," meant only for their ears. So Esau went out the door with a spring in his step and a smile on his lips. He made his way across the wilderness, tracked a prize deer, downed it, and confidently, quietly made his way back to his father's tent. He stepped into the room where his father was propped up on a pillow and whispered to him.

"Father, I'm here! And with your favorite dish!"

But his father didn't act glad to see him. He didn't look hungry. Instead, his father said, "Who?" as if he weren't expecting him.

"It's me, Father," he said impatiently, "with the food you asked for!"

Then Esau learned that someone else had been there in his absence. He discovered that the blessing was gone and all he would get, if anything, would be leftovers.

He roared in surprise and anguish. Who was the scoundrel that had cheated him? It was his brother Jacob.

His father said, "Your brother came with subtlety, and has taken away your blessing."

Esau spit out the words in bitterness. "Is not he rightly named Jacob? for he has supplanted me these two times: he took away my birthright; and, behold, now he hath taken away my blessing."

Now, the word *supplant* is used to describe someone tripping another in a race or battle, using a trick to win.

Let's see if this is so. Did Jacob trick him into selling his birthright or did he do it knowingly? What does God say about what happened that day? Hebrews 12:16 says Esau was an immoral and godless person who sold his own birthright for a single meal.

Then we see something else in Hebrews 12:17: "Afterwards, when he desired to inherit the blessing, he was rejected, for he found no place for repentance, though he sought for it with tears."

What is the difference between the birthright and blessing? The birthright was naturally his by birth, a title of privilege. The blessing was the father confirming it and officially conferring it upon him. Basically, the birthright and blessing were two parts of the same thing. The two could not be separated, but this did not stop Esau from trying!

What happened that day was Jacob cashing in on a promise Esau had made years ago and wanted to forget! I bet Esau had never told his father about the transaction years ago. He was just going to skate in and get the blessing after he had shunned it for a bowl of beans a long time ago. But God didn't take his flippant choice so lightly. Though Esau tried to separate the two, God tied the two together. The blessing was not his. God had recorded the transaction in the books of heaven. Underneath the heavenly blessing, in that eternal accounts ledger, are these words: "Esau sold for a bowl of beans and a slice of bread."

Many souls want the benefits of God's blessing; but they aren't willing to "go hungry," as Esau should have, to keep it. They think that God's favor shouldn't cost them anything to get or keep. They should be able to do as they want, pursue their natural desires, and still reap the benefits of following God. But life doesn't work that way. It is true that God says, "You can have what you want." But, like the little guy in the carriage, will you be happy with what you get?

God always gives you what you want. But remember: "Be not deceived; God is not mocked: for whatsoever a man sows, that shall he also reap" (Galatians 6:7).

With this being said, we might want to pray this prayer:

> Oh God, help us to
> > abhor our appetites,
> > > distrust our desires,
> > > > grow wary of our own
> > > > wisdom!
> Help us to love You,
> > cherish Your designs,
> > > and trust Your ways, which are past
> > > finding out!

Psalm 37:4 says, "Delight yourself in the LORD, and he will give you the desires of your heart." Isn't that a much better path?

The Grace of Gravity
antagonism is essential to life!

O ne year I took a field trip to the Science Museum in Oklahoma City with my little girl, Brooklynn, and her class. As part of the tour, we were led into the darkened IMAX theatre, where we were mesmerized by the giant screen.

"Disaster hits when we do not have resistance—in every area of our existence!"

It sucked us in and made us see things up very close, such as the roiling clouds of smoke and fire from the blast-off of the shuttle and the pocked surface of the moon and other planets. As we watched this virtual tour of the dark reaches of space, I was treated to a secret from God that struck home down deep in my soul.

It involved something as simple as the exercise required of the astronauts to survive. Here it is: On Earth, gravity works against our muscles and bones every time we move; but in the weightless environment of space, astronauts lose muscle mass and bone density almost immediately, endangering their lives. Their only cure is resistance in the form of exercise up to two hours a day.

"We are continually seeking for the easy way out, trying to avoid the struggle and pain of life..."

It suddenly occurred to me that in order for us to survive spiritually on this earth, God allows us to face forces of resistance that affect everything we do.

We do not like the fall from a tree or a building, but every move we make is monitored by the merciful hand of gravity which continually conditions us so that we can survive.

We even see this principle at play in medicine. After prolonged immobility, such as extended bed rest or having a body part in a cast, the muscles and bones begin to shrink from non-use. This process is called atrophy.

My point?

Antagonism is essential to life and survival!

This truth is illustrated in a thousand ways. Only through struggle is a baby born into this world: mammals by the pains of birth, birds and others by pecking through the egg shell. Even a caterpillar must struggle to become a butterfly.

Disaster hits when we do not have resistance – in every area of our existence!

Oswald Chambers claimed:

"The basis of physical, mental, moral, spiritual life is antagonism.

"Physical health is the balance between physical life and external nature, maintained only by sufficient vitality on the inside against things on the outside. Everything outside my physical life is designed to put me to death. Things which keep me going when I am alive disintegrate me when I am dead. If I have enough fighting power, I produce the balance of health.

"We don't even want to consider the fact that we may be in this fight for the long haul."

"Mental health: If I want to maintain a vigorous mental life, I have to fight; and from this fighting with life's questions and struggles, principles and convictions are produced. Only if I keep in the game of reaching and learning does my brain survive and thrive.

"The Christian walk is a struggle of new life, and life being established!'"

"Moral health: Everything that does not partake of the nature of virtue is the enemy of virtue in me, and it depends on what moral caliber I have whether I overcome and produce virtue. When I fight, I am moral in that particular. *No man is virtuous because he cannot help it; virtue is acquired."*

> "When we avoid the legitimate suffering that results from dealing with problems, we also avoid growth that problems demand from us"

We are continually seeking for the easy way out, trying to avoid the struggle and pain of life, longing secretly for the rest that shall one day be given us in eternity.

A cartoon shows a little boy in the car watching his dad outside in the pouring rain, fixing a flat tire. The boy has the window down and is asking his father why this is happening to them. The father looks at the boy and says, "Son, don't you understand? This is life. This is what is happening. We *can't* switch to another channel!"

A gardener took great pride in his lawn. One year his lawn was besieged with dandelions. He tried everything and still couldn't get rid of them. He wrote the Department of Agriculture, explaining all the different dandelion deterrents he had tried and asking what he should do next. The answer came back from the Department of Agriculture: "Try getting used to them!"

We are all like the man who had hitchhiked from coast to coast and had walked many miles in the process. He was asked what he had found the most difficult to endure. To the surprise of his questioner, it was not the steep mountains or the dazzling sun or the scorching desert heat that had troubled him. In the words of the traveler, "It was the sand in my shoe."

The grit of life irritates all of us, and there is nothing we can do about it except to stop intermittently, take off the sandal, and shake it out!

A quick and easy victory is what we desire: an escape from the long, arduous struggle. We don't even want to consider the fact that we may be in this fight for the long haul.

"... antagonism designed by God to produce a result not possible by any other process."

In the Civil War, the first Battle of Bull Run powerfully illustrated this human tendency. In the three months since the attack on Fort Sumter, there had been only small-scale clashes between the two sides. Abraham Lincoln decided to strike first. The Union strategy was to deal a crushing blow to Confederate forces near Manassas, Virginia, and quickly march on Richmond, the Confederate capital. The Northerners were pretty sure this

"I take pleasure in infirmities, in reproaches, in necessities, in persecutions, in distresses for Christ's sake: for when I am weak, then am I strong!"

would be the first—and last—significant battle of the war, and they wanted to see the action for themselves. Hundreds of people, including reporters, government officials, and even average citizens, traveled out to watch the battle. They made a day of it, bringing picnic lunches and wine, almost as if they were attending a modern-day tailgate party.

But they were in for a surprise.

These naïve spectators witnessed 850 deaths, and by the end of the day another 4,000 men were missing or wounded. The Union defeat was a huge shock to the North, which had been sure of its massive military and moral advantage. It took the shattered Union Army nearly thirty-six hours to get back to Washington, D.C., marching almost without rest or food.

"I take pleasure in infirmities, for Christ's sake: for when I am weak, then am I strong!'"

As one soldier put it, "This army that was supposed to crush the Confederates limped back into the capital more dead than alive."

Some in the South rejoiced over the triumph at Bull Run, which they felt proved that a Confederate soldier was the equal of any Union soldier, while others shared the feeling of most Northerners: this was going to be a very long war.

What a dark day it is for most Christians when they realize, as the Union and Confederacy did so long ago, that the battle they find themselves waging is going to be a long one.

Life is full of thorns that prick, rocks that bruise the feet, and words that stab the heart. We face heavy, storm-laden skies and swollen, nearly un-crossable streams. From the beginning when Pandora opened that tempting box of secrets, the world has been filled with haunting things and terrors and irritations to the soul, body, and mind. From the first plucking of the forbidden fruit, a dark something has spread in the waters of man's soul and flowed out to the world to create an atmosphere in which we are tested and tried from every possible angle. As much as its existence is hated, it is actually the key to our survival. It is *the grace of gravity!*

Percy Trueblood said, "Occasionally we talk of our Christianity as something that solves problems; there is a sense in which it does. Long before it does so, however, it increases both the number and intensity of problems!" The Christian walk is a struggle of new life, and life being established!

When we try to avoid problems and trials instead of facing them head-on with the grace and power of God, we get into trouble. Thomas A Kempis said, "All saints passed through man's tribulations and temptations and profited thereby. They that could not bear temptations became reprobate and fell away. Many seek to fly temptations and fall more grievously into them."

"Don't quit on God!" "We must be vigilant . . . because there are many subtle ways in which we can give up on God."

This effort to escape problems is hurting people in every facet of society. A lady in Oklahoma was sentenced to many years in prison for killing two people while driving drunk. What incriminated her was a phrase she had texted just before the crash: "Too drunk to care!" Her efforts to escape had landed her in a much more terrible position.

In *The Road Less Traveled*, Scott Peck, M.D., writes, "The tendency to avoid problems and emotional suffering inherent in them is the primary basis of all human mental illness. Some go to great lengths, creating a world of layered fantasies in which to live to the point of totally excluding reality. Others procrastinate, forget problems, pretend they do not exist, and even take drugs to assist in ignoring them, so that by deadening themselves to the pain they can forget the problems that cause the pain.

"When we avoid the legitimate suffering that results from dealing with problems, we also avoid growth that problems demand from us. In chronic mental illness we stop growing, become stuck, and begin to shrivel."

"They are spiritually more at home in the cemetery than in the green fields and flowers of life!"

This principle applies to every aspect of life.

Not only is antagonism necessary to our survival, it is also necessary for our success! Problems are the cutting edge that distinguishes between success and failure. Only in facing problems do we grow mentally and spiritually. Through the pain of confronting and resolving problems, we learn.

Enterprise, Alabama, was known for a long time as the Peanut Capital of the World. It became the peanut capital after boll weevils had eaten up all the cotton in the county. Poverty, want, and suffering followed in the wake of the boll weevil. But there came a time when Enterprise erected a monument to the boll weevil because it had forced the people to grow a variety of crops. One businessman in Miami said, "The boll weevil ate up my college education, but I am not complaining because I got an education the hard way and found my talents lay in the business world." He amassed a million dollar fortune and was so

> "Judge, they didn't send me here to quit. They didn't send me here to win. They sent me here to run this mile, and I ran the mile."

thankful for the boll weevil that he helped erect the boll weevil monument in Enterprise!

A man went into a beautifully appointed office of a successful manufacturer and later told this story:

"While I waited for the owner to answer a call, my attention was attracted to a picture on his desk. It was a photograph of a vicious-looking, ugly man. I wondered why anyone would want such a face staring at him continually. I asked him when he got off the phone if this was one of his friends.

"He said, 'Friend! Not on your life! That's the meanest man I ever knew on earth, and I used to work for him. I keep his picture here to remind me that if I don't make a success of this business, I have got to go back to work for that guy!'"

Acts 14:22 says that we must "through **much tribulation** enter into the kingdom of God"; and 1 Peter

4:12-16 adds, "Think it not strange concerning the fiery trial which is to try you, as though some strange thing happened unto you!"

What we face is antagonism designed by God to produce a result not possible by any other process. We look upon sin, the devil, and the forbidden tree as only evil—and they are if we let them destroy us—but they are also the fires that transform ore into silver, gold, and steel. They are the very stuff God uses to make saints out of babies!

George Matheson, the well-known blind preacher of Scotland, said, "My God, I have never thanked Thee for my 'thorn'! I have thanked Thee a thousand times for my roses, but never once for my 'thorn'; I have been looking forward to a world where I shall get compensation for my cross, but I have never thought of my cross as itself a present glory. Teach me the glory of my cross; teach me the value of my 'thorn.' Show me that I have climbed to Thee by the path of pain. Show me that my tears have made my rainbow."

Paul testified of his thorn in 2 Corinthians 12:8-10: "For this thing I sought the Lord thrice, that it might depart from me. And he said unto me, 'My grace is sufficient for thee: for my strength is made perfect in weakness.' Most gladly therefore will I rather glory in my infirmities, that the power of Christ may rest upon me…I take pleasure in infirmities, in reproaches, in necessities, in persecutions, in distresses for Christ's sake: for when I am weak, then am I strong!"

Don't quit on God! Christ was tempted in all points and never "quit" on God; and as His followers, we should do the same. We must be vigilant because there are many subtle ways in which we can give up on God.

Charles Allen said, "I know a young lady who was in an automobile wreck. She was thrown into the windshield, and the glass cut her face severely. When I first saw her in the hospital, she was so thankful and grateful that her life had been spared. The wreck was very serious, and it was a miracle that she had not been killed. She expressed gratitude to God for her life and felt that because God had spared her life, she wanted to live for others as she had never done before. However, later on she would look at those scars on her face. The surgeons did a good job in minimizing the scars, but still they were there and she felt disfigured. Actually, the disfigurement was not nearly as severe as it grew to be in her mind. That is true many times of our problems. They have a way of growing out of proportion, as we continue to think of them. Gradually, she emphasized less and less her gratitude to God for being saved, and more and more the resentment she had over those scars on her face." She was quitting.

Years ago tradition dictated that when a husband died, a widow should wear black, withdraw from life, and observe what was called "mourning."

I have seen a few people who have come through the Valley of the Shadow of Death but have never removed their mourning clothes. Death is with them, like a ghostly pallor. You touch their spiritual cheeks and they are cold. You hear them speak and it is always of the past. They are spiritually more at home in the cemetery than in the green fields and flowers of life! They have quit, and are "dead men walking."

May we never quit, no matter the struggle!

C Roy Angell tells the following story as he heard it from Dr. John Maguire, who was at that time the executive secretary for the Florida Baptist Convention. Dr. Maguire was also a high school track coach.

"I took the track team down to the state meet one year and saw a most unusual and wonderful thing. The men were lining up for the mile race which, of course, was the big event of the track meet. Since it was rumored that the state record for the mile might be broken that day, an unusually large crowd of spectators had gathered. One of the schools had a most promising miler. Twice at other events he had come within a second of the state record, and he was out to break it this time. As they gathered around the starting mark, all eyes were on that tall, good-looking young man with a gracious smile on his face. He was long of limb and with all the marks of an athlete of the first magnitude.

"Then I saw at the far end of the starting line a boy who was in every way a sharp contrast to this athlete. He was small of stature, his shoulders were bent a little, he was hollow-chested, and even his legs were not straight. I wondered why in the world a school would put a boy like that into the mile race to run against that splendid athlete. The command came to 'toe your mark, get set.' Then the pistol cracked and the race was on.

"The fine athlete sprang into the lead at the very beginning, and with every lap he widened the distance between himself and the others. The little fellow steadily fell behind. When they came into the home stretch, the athlete sprinted the last hundred yards. As he broke the tape, a deafening roar went up from the crowd. He had broken the state record! Only a few others finished the mile; most of the runners had dropped out when they saw it was hopeless for them to win.

"As the field crew were bringing out the hurdles to set up for the next race, suddenly one of the judges yelled, 'Get those hurdles out of the way. This race is not over. Look!'

"Around the turn came that little boy, panting and staggering. Everybody in the audience stood silently and watched as he dragged up that last hundred yards and literally fell across the finish line. His face ground into the cinder track. One of the judges ran and turned him over on his back, took his handkerchief, and wiped the blood off his face.

"The judge asked him, 'Son, why didn't you drop out back yonder? What are you doing in the mile race, anyway?'

"Between gasps for breath, the boy answered, 'My school had a good miler, but he got sick two or three days ago and couldn't run. The coach had promised to have a man in every event, so he asked me if I'd come and run the mile.'

"'Well, son,' the judge continued, 'Why didn't you just drop out, quit way back there? You were over half a lap behind.'

"He answered, 'Judge, they didn't send me here to quit. They didn't send me here to win. **They sent me here to run this mile, and I ran the mile.'**"

Run the mile! God didn't save you to quit. God didn't save you to "win" against the competition. He put you on this earth to "run the mile", so *run the mile*!

A Delayed Payday
the reward is on its way

"It does not pay to be true to your conviction, to the highest standard that you know in a time of crisis. It is too much trouble." This is what Satan tells every Christian.

Joseph faced this conundrum for years after rejecting Potiphar's wife. It seemed true. Because he stood for his principles, he paid a very high price for a very long time before God finally rewarded him.

This is the case with many Christians. The devil has plenty of time to work on his end, arguing against God in the interim between our stand and God's reward. This is the testing ground. This is when we ask ourselves

Does God see? Does He care? Does it really pay off to be faithful?

To hear the devil, it doesn't. To look at circumstances, it doesn't.

This is where Joseph's story fits in so powerfully. His experience tells of God's remunerating him for being true when all circumstances argued against it.

First of all, let's address the choice Joseph made.

Joseph had had a rather rough and tumble journey up this point in his life. Oh, he had enjoyed the favor of Dad, but along with this he had been shunned by his brothers and then sold into slavery. He had traveled a long way in a gypsy-like caravan to Egypt, with no hope of ever seeing Dad and home again. He had eked out an existence, and through faithfulness he had caught the eye of Potiphar, captain of the guard. He enjoyed relative success, and each day brought greater appreciation for his presence and his contribution to the bottom line of his master's finances. It was beginning to be a win-win for all. But this all changed quite rapidly, and it wasn't due to his messing up or being untrue. He had problems *because* he was true to his master!

Enter with me into the palatial estate of Potiphar, past fluted pillars and splashing fountains, into shiny marble halls lined with gold-gilded paintings. Here is Joseph at a large table, poring over numbers and giving instructions to the constant retinue of servants. God has blessed his hand. He has been able to figure out the most challenging problems of Potiphar's business and turn them into a success, but he is about to run into one problem for which he has no "smooth" answer. He isn't going to be able to talk his way out of this one.

This is how it happened. He caught not only the eye of his master, but also the eye of his master's wife, for totally different reasons.

I really do wonder why she picked on him. The obvious answer is that he was strikingly handsome. Why wouldn't a woman want him? But, why did she want him now? He had obviously been around for at least a little while, enough time to catch the eye of Potiphar, enough time to rise through the ranks, enough time for Potiphar's holdings to increase dramatically from Joseph's wisdom and integrity. So we might ask her, "Why now, honey?"

Did you notice that it wasn't until after he was promoted to the top position that she set her eye upon him? From what I understand, many women are drawn to men of power, be it politicians, policemen, or preachers. Is this what happened here?

She had an eye for beauty and appreciated a young man in the prime of his life with a sharp mind. He could be used to her advantage. He could be her next plaything. Sure, he was a little prudish, but that could be overcome with a little time. He was from a different background, with morals obviously much different from those of his

> ". . . until God is ready for us to come out, we are staying in! False justice will prevail until the time is right."

current surroundings; but with a few encouraging words and subtle advances, he could and would come around to her way of thinking.

So, she approached him, tried to get him alone, told him how much she appreciated his faithfulness to her husband's estate. She engineered times to be in the house near him when the others servants were out. She expressed her admiration for him and supported him in his business and was close by to help in any way she could. He doubtless appreciated this show of affection and support from the master's wife. Things were going well.

But then he began to feel ill at ease around her. Her looks and laughs and presence made him uncomfortable, especially in light of what Potiphar might think if he knew his wife was giving so much attention to Joseph. We are not sure how it happened, but somehow she managed to invite him into her bedroom to share an intimacy with him that should be shared only with her husband.

Immediately Joseph responded with an absolute "No!" He had tried to avoid her. He had tried to brush off her praise that was applied a little too thickly. He had tried to ignore the lingering glances, but this was too much.

He then reasoned with her. He threw himself upon the mercy of her conscience. "Can't you see that it would be dishonorable to betray the trust of the very man who has put me where I am? Can't you see that I cannot do this wickedness against my God?"

But she would have none of it, for wickedness in a heart never does things "reasonably" but selfishly. How many have I seen who forged on ahead to do or get what they wanted, even in the face of betraying people's trust and ruining homes and careers and ministries?

She pressed him daily. She had time and she would use it to her advantage. Where was he to go? He was a slave. It seemed he had no options. He was stuck. How many find themselves in a similar predicament?

Perhaps she thought that he was naïve or just scared. Perhaps she believed that he just needed more time away from his roots to be able to drift in his convictions and thinking.

All the devil needs with many people is just a little time to change their views. You can take a snapshot of them today and another twenty years later and you will see this clearly. Over time, Satan can do what he could not do at the time of their original stand. Oh, that constant, silent pressure--pressure from a loved one, a spouse, or even a child.

But Joseph was different. Instead of eroding under pressure, he took measures to protect his original stand and grew ever stronger for it. Scripture tells us he avoided her. He probably did not treat her rudely, but he silently tried to put up barriers between them, barriers that only the two of them would catch and understand. This is extremely important. Though others may be oblivious to your interaction, you know in your heart what you are doing; and to be true, you must decisively take all precautions to stop any illicit or wrong friendship.

Finally, tired of this cat and mouse pursuit, she forced a head-on collision. No matter how hard Joseph tried, he could not reason eloquently enough or find enough ways to avoid the issue. She found her moment. She trapped him. Gripping his coat with whitened knuckles, she demanded his cooperation. She could not stand being resisted, spurned, and denied what she wanted so badly.

"You see, God always gets to write the last chapter, not Potiphar's wife."

Now what was Joseph to do? He was trapped. There was no way out the back door, no silent exit possible. It was "face it head on"–and he did.

Joseph didn't crumble in that moment. He ran. He became radical. He did not stroll out. He shot out! W. M. Tidwell, a great pastor of yesteryear, said, "A good run is better than a poor stand!"

He escaped! Praise the Lord! Where? Right into the rabbit hole of "righteous anger," false accusations, prison and infamy. Sometimes deliverance from the hand of Satan is not pleasant. The pressure doesn't ease; it gets worse.

Humor me a moment. Let's study his choice a little more, from the devil's perspective. Poor Joseph. He just didn't know how to "get along" with others sometimes. He didn't know which side of an issue to take so that he was applauded instead of flogged, promoted instead of imprisoned.

It is interesting how many people, in an hour of crisis, will study a situation to see which side will afford them the greater personal advantage.

It is interesting how many will instinctively choose the side which will cost them the least. That's the side for them. People who operate by choosing the least collateral damage over principle will also put that pressure on others.

This kind of tough spot is a familiar place to many.

Pastors take a holy stand while trying to be kind and still end up losing church members and salaries. Many in the work of the Lord see their reputation and ministry at risk in these moments. For others, relationships with families and friends are endangered if they make the "wrong" move. Job promotions or even job security weighs in the balance.

We might ask, "Joseph, did you realize just who you were standing up to?" Though Potiphar's wife did not rule the house, she *was* the master's wife! He could have taken this into account. He could easily have justified cooperating with her.

Can't you just hear the other servants?

"He should have just slept with her. He should have become part of the fabric of Potiphar's house and behaved himself 'wisely.' He should have respected the power structure and done his duty as a servant. Who was he to defy the will of the woman of the house? What a stupid man."

He could have avoided a head-on collision. But now, instead of acceptance and promotion (albeit with a guilty conscience), he paid dearly for his stand for years.

This is how it happened.

That sweet, soft-voiced woman with her touch of velvet became a shrill harpy with bared talons, ready to draw blood. Joseph was up against a very dark and dirty power, a power which had soothingly tried to win his affection. We all have seen it. The power that promises promotions, positions, and other rewards of all kinds is the same power that can tear us down in an instant if we defy it.

She immediately switched her roles, from the aggressor to the innocent victim. How quickly people can switch roles. Now she pretended that she was actually the one standing for morality! Have you ever been around those who can so quickly adopt a good cause or righteous principle whenever convenient, all the while focused upon attacking an innocent person? It is always healthy to make sure our deepest motives are pure.

Watch her posture as the innocent one in retaliation. It is time to destroy the one who would not "see it her way." She is now crying and being consoled by the attending staff. Potiphar comes through the door and finds her makeup running and eyes swollen from crying. Instantly perching on the edge of the couch in a consoling manner, he listens with astonishment at the wild tale of his prized steward betraying his trust by assaulting his beautiful, innocent wife. I can hear her whimper through muffled sobs something about how disappointed and shocked she is with Joseph. How helpless she was. How she fought back when forced by him. She then turns to the men of the house who had come running the first time; and they corroborate her story as witnesses, even though they weren't there when it happened. They obviously knew on which side to stand!

Imagine the gossip which flew out on wings of fire about how far Joseph had fallen. It was so sad, enraging even. But it was *very good news,* the kind that was juicy and sweet to the taste, that raised eyebrows, and that made people catch their breath and shake their head. I'm sure they had heard much good about Joseph, but this bad was just too delectable a fruit to ignore. It made them feel better about themselves as they pondered the decline of the rest of the world.

I'm sure all the guard under Potiphar's charge and even Pharaoh heard of it. All the high society ladies' circles heard the offended party's story and consoled her. Here he was, trusted with the highest position and betraying that trust! Every friendly face that had ever loved him, patted him on the back, or praised him now said his name with a hiss and discussed his crime repeatedly. Why, it even filtered through the grates to the prisons below. They all knew what a Judas, a Benedict Arnold he was.

What happened to Joseph as a result of this false charge of crime committed?

Potiphar flew into a rage. He did not ask Joseph his side of the story. The evidence was there. There was no arguing. The lady of the house had spoken.

Potiphar, how you must feel betrayed! How smooth Joseph was to trick you, to get in close and then destroy you! He was a low-down, dirty dog for taking advantage of your trust! Of course he goes to prison!

But if Potiphar had thought for a minute, he would have remembered Joseph's faithfulness. He would have known that Joseph was not capable of such a crime.

Did Potiphar lightly put Joseph in that position? No. But he was caught up in the moment. And it was easier to deal with a servant than a wife! So Joseph must go.

In case you don't know it, the truth is that you won't win the Nobel Peace Prize every time you choose to stand for your convictions. People will not always flock to praise you for your ideals. You will even be resented. You will "fall" in the eyes of many for your stand. You will be rewarded for being true with hatred and punishment from those closest to you. There will be tremendous pressure from the majority to see it their way. There will also be promotions and praise in hand for those who finally acquiesce. But Joseph didn't.

So off to the prison he went. No more Joseph – a problem fixed. Can you imagine the sense of accomplishment and vindication when Potiphar and his wife dusted their hands from making Joseph pay for his petulance and betrayal? The story was *over,* according to them. While they never seemed to pay for her sin and Potiphar's injustice, Joseph suffered for years from their mistreatment. Many times the harm we commit against others does not bother us nearly as much as it does them. Why? We were on the pommel end of the sword. He who is wounded will feel the wound and scar much longer than we will. We ask, "Why don't they just get over it?" because we didn't feel a thing!

Poor Joseph. Look at him. He does not see the bright future awaiting him. He sees only dark tunnels, dirty prisoners, forlorn faces, and scurrying rats for years and years and years.

"It does not pay to be true to your convictions, to stand on principle, Joseph," seems to echo through the corridors of his new underground home.

But God's Word has a different story to tell in Psalm 105:17-22: "God sent a man before Israel, even Joseph, who was sold for a servant: Whose feet they hurt with fetters: he was laid in iron: Until the time that his word came: the word of the LORD tried him. The king sent and loosed him; even the ruler of the people, and let him go free. He made him lord of his house, and ruler of all his substance: To bind his princes at his pleasure; and teach his senators wisdom."

The Psalmist says that his soul was in iron until the time God released him. I'm sure he relived every action and wondered if he could have done anything differently.

He definitely tried to get out in his own way but found that no matter how he tried to straighten out things and get justice, his plans didn't work. We need to learn the same lesson: until God is ready for us to come out, we are staying in! False justice will prevail until the time is right.

How did he finally get out?

Ironically, Potiphar locked him in the *same prison where the king's prisoners were found.* Was that an accident? God put him in that place for a reason: someone in Pharaoh's house remembered him for the same gift he had evidenced in the prison. You see, even in prison, his spirit shone like a lighthouse across the troubled waters of men's souls.

Then God sent a man who unlocked his cell and cleaned him up; and before he knew what was happening, he was standing in the glaring light of day and before the glory of Pharaoh himself. The Dreamer was asked if he could interpret dreams. God gave Pharaoh a mystery to solve and then gave Joseph the only key that would unlock that mystery!

GOD unlocked the cell. GOD promoted him. GOD vindicated him!

Where are you now, Joseph?

"I am really busy! I have servants running everywhere. We are buying supplies for the coming famine. Pharaoh has given me his ring and bought me a house and a golden chariot. Princes are bowing before me and my power is astonishing!"

Did Potiphar ever apologize to Joseph for what he had done to him unfairly? Did his wife ever come clean? We don't have that record.

But we do see that God took Joseph past the demotion of Potiphar and promoted him above his former master; and Potiphar, if alive, knew *exactly* who Joseph was. Do you think Potiphar remembered what he had done? I believe he walked the floors at night, saw his possessions dwindle, and knew in his heart that he had wronged a loyal friend.

Does it pay to stay true to your highest convictions, or is it better to take the easy way out and side with what appears to be the quick advantage?

Ask Joseph. Ask yourself. Ask God.

You see, God always gets to write the last chapter, not Potiphar's wife.

Playing Chess with God

"Think you can figure out what God is up to?"

One of my most vivid memories with my Grandfather Boice is poring over a chess board with him... from opposite ends. Granddad was a student of chess. He would check out books from the library and study moves like chess was a science, and it worked for him! My boy David is an avid chess player. He thinks ahead and usually beats me soundly. He is a difficult opponent, and I am wary when he invites me to a game of chess; for it is a grueling ordeal, involving large amounts of time straining the brain to figure out his end game.

"Trying to figure out what God is doing with our lives is like playing chess . . ."

Trying to figure out what God is doing with our lives is like playing chess with these guys. We watch every move and wonder what He is up to. We try to guess his next move. It is a very taxing occupation. To make it harder, He is not looking over our shoulder, encouraging us. Instead, He seems to be our opponent; and opponents are very silent, hiding their true intentions, which are presumed to be disastrous to our own purposes and well- being.

"It is never fun to play chess with God"

When I read the book of Job, I am reminded of the game of chess. I see God on one side (along with the Devil), and I see Job on the other. Job has a coterie of advisors (his wife and friends), and together they are all trying to figure out what God is up to in this horrid game. It is never fun to play chess with God.

We all know the story of how Job lost everything in a sweep of surprise attacks that turned his world upside down. It is obvious that serving God was rewarding until the clouds rolled in and life refused to give him the gifts he had always assumed were rightly his. Most of this book is a scene of Job on the ash heap, covered in painful sores, searching for a God he thought loved Him, arguing with friends who only darkened counsel with their words, and feebly holding on to his integrity as he scraped himself with broken pottery and wished for the merciful sleep of death. Life held no glimmer for him; it only mocked him. We see how heaven looked on in silence and the Devil brooded nearby, straining at his divine leash, to break down the integrity of Job. What an awful scene.

In the pain of this moment I would like for us to examine the guessing that went on from Job's side of the chess board, trying to figure out what was happening to him.

"... he begins to wonder if God cares about what he cares about."

Let us examine Job's response first. Why is God doing this? Job begins to question the purpose of his existence, to wonder why he was even born, to wonder why God doesn't just let him die and get the pain over with. There seems to be no good reason for his suffering. Look at all the times of joy: when he was born, when he was blessed for his faithfulness, when he was honored by others. But that is all gone now, and there seems to be no purpose in the emptiness. Life is a mockery.

There is no doubt in his mind that God is just and sovereign. The Lord gives and takes away. Blessed be the name of the Lord. But he begins to wonder if God cares about what he cares about. He begins to wonder if his dreams and wishes really matter to God, considering what has happened. He begins to wonder if all his righteous living has really been worth it.

Job's situation reminds me of a story I read about Thorvaldsen, the great sculptor of the nineteenth century, who carved from white marble the most beautiful statue ever made of Jesus. The original is in Copenhagen and cannot be bought. It has been said that Thorvaldsen's Christ has channeled more than five million tourists through Copenhagen. One winter the Prince of Denmark invited him to be his guest at the winter palace for the season. Thorvaldsen accepted under the condition that he might bring with him the piece of marble on which he was presently working. He felt he could not afford to waste that much time, for there were so many pieces of sculpture in his creative mind. The prince responded with no hesitation.

"Not only may you bring it, but I'll send for it."

His prince set up a studio for him in the winter palace. Thorvaldsen worked every day, even into the night. One morning, at a late breakfast, he and the prince looked out through the big picture window at the children making a snowman. They had borrowed the prince's long cutaway coat, his high silk hat, his cane, his pipe and his glasses. All went well until they tried to make a face to resemble their handsome prince. Finally, they gave up. Seeing their downcast faces, the prince turned to his guest.

"Job's wife never doubts Job's integrity like his friends. She in turn begins to question God!"

"You're the master sculptor of the world. Don't you want to go out and help them just a little?"

Thorvaldsen was a perfectionist. He put on his boots and his heavy coat and went out to help make the snowman's face. He asked the prince to stand at the window where he could see him. After packing the snow into a hard ball, he took a sharp chisel and carved out a perfect likeness. It took him three hours. He caught cold and went to bed. That night everything froze. The next morning the sun shone brightly

"To many like Job's wife, God is more trouble than He is worth!"

and soon the delicately chiseled face and features of the prince were all blurred. The next day when the weather turned warm, the snowman melted and drooped, entirely destroying the likeness. It was, as Shakespeare said, "Love's labors lost."

Thorvaldsen stayed in bed nearly five weeks with pneumonia, for there was no penicillin in those days. What a great cost, to suffer so long for an accomplishment that was so short lived. What a waste of effort!

I believe Job felt the same way. He did not curse God, but he surely cursed the day he was born and the day in which he currently lived. He was in pain, not thinking straight and not accepting comfort. Many have been there.

The next one I would bring into the picture is Job's wife. See her trying to guess what God is up to on the chess board of life. She never doubts Job's integrity like his friends do, for she has lived with him and knows him well. In fact, she knows him so well that she in turn begins to question God! Her husband doesn't deserve such cruel treatment.

We are not given much information about her, but the snapshot we do have tells us much. I assume she has been a faithful wife who attended church with her husband every time, who sat with bowed head at the dinner table and with gratitude thanked God for the blessings of life, and who very much enjoyed being married to a man so successful in life, blessed by the God he served. It pains her much to watch her faithful husband be treated like this. She feels he has been betrayed. She watches him suffer, groan, weep, and writhe. It is madness to her to watch such an intensely emotional scene, to see the one she loves suffer at the hands of a silent God. This latest move on the chess board is terrible and really shows the heart of God: that He has been playing all along with Job and that Job's allegiance really has meant nothing to Him at all. What a God! The solution to this endless pain is simple: Quit the God who is toying with him and give up the will to live. End the suffering.

"Here is a group of men who believe in God, or what they think they know about God. The truth is that they are not loyal to God as much as they are to their opinions about God"

To many like Job's wife, God is more trouble than He is worth! Get mixed up with Him and your life could go sour quickly! Why take the chance? Quit this thing called faith in God and live a more predictable, comfortable life.

The last group of "chess- playing advisors" are the friends of Job. Let's see what they make of this last move of God on Job. I see them look in horror upon the destroyed lands, the charred remains, the empty fields, the freshly dug graves of his children, the moaning wife pacing the halls of their great house, and the agony of Job's physical and emotional pain. It is too much for them. Surely, there is an explanation for this... this awful tragedy and surprise. They never doubt the heart of God like Job's wife does. No, they question the integrity of Job! They thought they knew Job, but his companion, Eliphaz, elucidates their unanimous conviction:

"Of all people, we never dreamed this of you. You were the example to all of how to live, the encourager of the downtrodden, the lifter up of people's heads. Now we see that you are being stricken of God."

Here is a group of men who believe in God, or what they think they know about God. The truth is that they are not loyal to God as much as they are to their opinions about God, and though they do not understand Job, they are willing to de-Christianize him in order to hold tightly to their convictions.

Trouble is ripe ground for surmise. Many Christians are like the heathen who guess the gods are mad when something bad happens like famine or plague and believe the gods are happy when the harvest is good, the rain pours down, the enemies are quiet, and precious life is protected. They live in superstition. But this is part of the trial: to face people who turn from you in suspicion, who can't be blessed when you are because you are a "hypocrite." They cannot

> ". . . this is part of the trial: to face people who turn from you in suspicion, who can't be blessed when you are because you are a 'hypocrite.'"

bear to listen to you pray, preach, or testify because of the "awful sin" you have supposedly committed. These people are like Elihu, David's brother, who "knew the naughtiness of David's heart." Such perception. Such divine wisdom! How easily the "discerning ones" can tell you who you really are and ask you to quit the charade.

"God is too great to be explained, to be discussed, to be analyzed, or to be complained against by man"

No, Job's comforters are not at all questioning God's integrity. They are after Job. It cannot be for "no purpose" that God is doing this to Job. Contrarily, it is for a specific purpose all this trouble has come. It must be some secret sin. Eliphaz even goes so far as to claim he has had a special vision, a revelation about Job. It came in the night and his hair stood up on end. When Job insists that he has done nothing to bring this upon himself, they become very indignant, motivated, and ready to fight for the

"And the funny thing is, both sides won!"

cause of righteousness. It reminds me of Isaiah's text, "We did esteem him (Christ) stricken of God!"

Finally, God speaks up. God's answer is nothing like what has been posed by the others. The great Chess Player speaks. He does not explain His moves or answer the questions Job has asked of Him. He does not initially tell Job why he lost his wealth, family, and health. He answers with questions to Job which bring him to his knees. He asks him if he remembers when God flung stars from His fingertips and hung the moon out for a night light, to which Job admits he does not. God says, "My point exactly."

He then gives Job a tour of His creation, speaking of the oceans and restless power that is reined in by Himself, and asks Job if he remembers helping God with their creation. Again Job replies that he does not remember. God answers, "My point exactly."

Then he asks Job if he recalls when God made the great monster of the sea that defies the heavy hand of man's authority, a creature so great that it makes all mankind flee in terror. Job confesses he does not remember that. God answers, "My point exactly."

God answers Job with questions that help Job realize how wise and beyond comprehension God's ways and wisdom are. He implies something by this exchange.

"Job," He says, "though you cannot understand all that I have done and am doing, I want you to trust me. Trust me that I care about every day you live, every dream you dream, every sorrow you suffer. Trust me that, contrary to your wife's accusation, I will never leave nor forsake you, even when it seems as if I have. Trust me, contrary to your friends' suspicions, that even when you are going through hard times, it does not mean that I am angry with you because of some secret sin you have committed, but that I love you even then."

God is too great to be explained, to be discussed, to be analyzed, or to be complained against by man. God is to be obeyed and trusted, to be held to, even as Job said he would hold to him: "Though he slay me, yet will trust him."

One wet, foggy, muddy day, a little girl was standing on the side of a street in London, waiting for an opportunity to cross over. So she walked up and down, looking into the faces of those who passed by. Some looked careless, some appeared harsh, some were in haste, and she did not find the one she sought. At length an aged man, rather tall and spare, and of grave yet kindly aspect, came walking down the street. Looking into his face, she seemed to see the one for whom she had been waiting, and she went up to him and whispered timidly.

"Please, sir, will you help me over?"

The old man saw the little girl safely across the street, and when he afterward told the story he said that her trust in him was the greatest compliment he had ever received.

That man was Lord Shaftesbury. He had received honors at the hands of a mighty nation and was regarded highly by royalty; but the greatest compliment he ever had in his life was when that little unknown girl singled him out in the jostling crowd in a London street and dared to trust him, stranger though he was, to protect and assist her.

I believe Job began to see God in a different light that day. Overcome by the manifestation of God's glory, Job humbles himself and repents.

"I have heard of thee by the hearing of the ear; but now my eye seeth thee; wherefore I abhor myself, and repent in dust and ashes."

He repents not of sin, but of a lack of faith in his struggle with how God is playing the chess game of his life. He climbs back up into the lap of God and snuggles a little closer. God then points an angry finger at Job's comforters and demands they ask Job to pray for them. God then turns--and this means a u-turn--the direction of everything in Job's life and heads it back the other way! Job dies many years later, thanking God for such a rich life, after all!

"Ye have heard of the patience of Job, and have seen the end of the Lord, or the outcome of the Lord's dealings, that the Lord is very pitiful (extremely compassionate) and full of mercy" (Jas 5:10-11).

God proved that He did indeed care about Job, for He had put a hedge around him, protected his life from Satan, then rewarded him doubly for his sufferings. Job died at a good old age, full of gratitude for the life God had given him. It may have looked very bleak when God initially made His move, but the end of the game was worth it all.

And the funny thing is, both sides won!

A Night to Remember

"Why are ye fearful, O ye of little faith?"

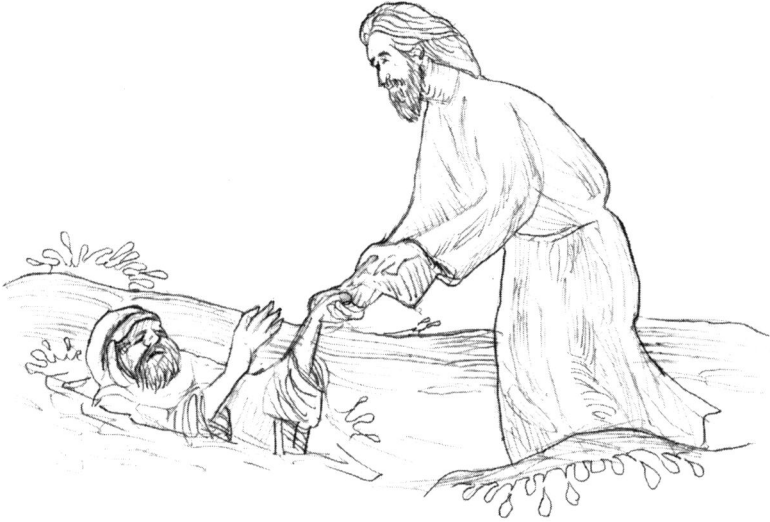

Then he arose, and rebuked the winds and the sea; and there was a great calm."

What a night for the disciples! A night they would never forget. A night *you* never would have forgotten either, if you had been with them!

Their story makes me think of

"They had left in the wake of their ministry no personality unmoved, no disease unhealed, no demon-possessed soul undelivered."

those on the *Titanic* who survived that horrible night. History tells us that many of the lifeboats put out from that great sinking ship were not half full. People by the hundreds were left behind to drown. A certain swimmer succeeded in making his way to one of these half-empty boats. He clutched the side and tried to climb in, but no one would help him. Not only so, but a woman took an oar and pounded his hands until he could cling no longer, and he dropped back to his death. Why did she do that? It was not because there was no room in the boat--there was plenty. She was brutalized by fear. It was a night never to be forgotten.

The disciples had their own memorable night, but it had a happier ending.

Let's go out down to the edge of the lapping water and join the fishermen as they are preparing to push out into the deep. The background of this night's story is absolutely necessary here. Christ had told the disciples to pass to the other side in their boat, in the evening. Now, usually the evening is not a good time to go skipping out across a lake; but *Jesus* had said it, and who were they to question Him?

"This storm became a very special storm-- not your normal storm."

I am sure they glanced at the sky with a suspicious, knowing look, being experienced sailors and all; but God was with them! They must have felt invincible. The glow of their success was unparalleled at this point. They had left in the wake of their ministry no personality unmoved, no disease unhealed, no demon-possessed soul undelivered. Without exception, those who sought Christ's touch had experienced it. And the disciples had witnessed it all.

Of course they would go to the other side! Confidently, they hoisted the sails, which flapped and popped in the brisk evening breeze. They pushed off; and, as suspected, the wind kicked up a steady pace which in a matter of minutes began to roll the waters, slapping their bark with white-capped waves and kicking up weeping walls of spray.

The sea beat a faster tempo, and they finally traded canvas for oars to steady the boat. With arms like corded bands of steel, they leaned into those oars with beating hearts, burning muscles, and eventually, failing spirits.

"Have you ever wanted to ask Christ some questions? What would you have said if you had been one of the disciples?"

This storm became a very special storm--not your normal storm. It seemed as if it were possessed of a spirit of darkness, intent upon taking them down, along with their Master. We know that later when Christ awoke, He rebuked the storm. Why *rebuke*? That is a rather strong word. Its root means "to size up or put something in its place." From this we get the idea of censuring or admonishing. Some things Christ rebuked in other settings shed light upon His action here:

He rebuked devils, and they departed from afflicted souls.

He rebuked Peter, saying, "Get thee behind me, Satan."

He rebuked the fever that raged in Simon's mother-in-law, and she arose and ministered to them.

It seems there must have been a spirit in the wind, a dark force behind it intent on taking them down. Perhaps for this reason, Christ *rebuked* the wind.

Have you ever been in a storm and suspected its maker was intent upon destroying you? Christ is aware of every storm that kicks up the sea around your little boat.

"Have you ever noticed that God never seems to respond to our circumstances the way we do?"

Let's go back to the disciples and watch as they continued to struggle against the sea as it picked up its pace and became more ominous. They probably began to think about Christ's wanting them to cross at this time of the day in this weather. It was bad timing at best. Then they started wondering about His wisdom and care. Where was He when they were struggling? He was no sailor; that was their job. But at least He could help!

Where was Christ?

Sleeping.

Their nerves were frayed. They were slipping and sliding on the deck. Out of resources, convinced this was their last voyage, they stormed into His sleeping chamber with a stinging question in their moment of desperation and struggle: "Do you not care that we perish?"

In other words, "Where have you been while we've been out here struggling against the storm?"

Or, "How could you be so senseless as to not understand the danger we are in at this very moment?"

Or, "You got us into this mess, and at least you could try to help us out."

Or, "You are pretty smart on land, but this time you have gotten us into a mess you can't get us out of; and to top it off, it doesn't seem you have any heart to feel our anxiety!"

Have you ever wanted to ask some questions to somebody who did you wrong? "You wait; when I see that person I'm going to ask him a thing or two." This is probably how Peter felt when he was searching for the One who had sent them on this fool voyage in the evening.

> "Humanity tends to ask questions and come up with conclusions that never help them."

Have you ever wanted to ask Christ some questions? What would you have said if you had been one of the disciples? What *have* you said when in your own storms?

Jesus awoke and gave two responses: one to the wind, one to the disciples.

He rebuked the wind, and then He rebuked the disciples:

"Why are you fearful, O ye of little faith?"

Now, that was odd. And rude. A little rough on the ego. Their feelings were a little frayed at the present, and that was no way to talk to someone in that condition.

Look at Him! Hear Him!

He didn't apologize for being asleep. He didn't pat them on the back consolingly, saying it was going to be

"OK." He didn't look for their gratitude when He calmed the storm. The whole ordeal ended in a strange silence. He certainly surprised them.

First, he stilled the storm. Of all the things they expected Him to do, stilling the storm was not on their list of predictions.

Then he asked them, "Why are you afraid, O ye of little faith?"

Have you ever noticed that God never seems to respond to our circumstances the way we do? He never seems to see things the way we see them. He never even seems to ask the "right" questions.

"Why are you afraid?" No one in a thousand years would have thought of that question. It was totally odd. We are supposed to be afraid in a storm. We are supposed to freak out and "lose our cool." We are human!

". . . the real issue of their heart is actually revealed by asking them some very different questions . . ."

But are we? Just human? I guess Christ expects something more than "human responses" from His followers. Perhaps He knows we have emotions, but that we ought to have enough trust in Him to be able to keep our spiritual equilibrium, poise, grace, and focus in the storm.

The disciples' query was very different from Christ's. They had said, "Do you not care that we are about to die?"

Humanity tends to ask questions and come up with conclusions that never help them. People ask questions that reveal more about themselves in a crisis than they do about the God they are questioning.

My boy Joshua came to me the other day with a question posed by his atheistic friends: "If God is in control and so kind, then why is there hunger in the world?" It seemed like a fair question. If God is in complete control of the world, then all famine must be a result of God's negligence. We could also say the same for war in the world: "If God is so kind and in control, then why is there war?" Of course, these questions can be answered with the following arguments:

> ". . . the questions humans ask reveal more about themselves than they do about God!"

Their question assumes people are not responsible for their own actions.

Their question denies the existence of dark forces at work. They fail to acknowledge that God is not the only spiritual presence active in the world.

Their question does not even start to grasp the bigger picture of what God allows for now and how He will ultimately deal with all injustice.

But the real issue of their heart is actually revealed by asking *them* some very different questions: "Why are you asking about the existence of a kind God?

Do you doubt His love? Are there not enough beauty and love and order and kindness in nature to argue for such a Creator? Or, do you simply desire an excuse to ignore God?"

Paul says clearly that there is enough proof in nature for men to believe and act according to the knowledge that there is a God; but they choose to doubt and ask impertinent questions, creating false struggles and fake arguments that lead them nowhere except to failure in life and eternity.

"... every jolt that brings forth what is inside in the form of a question—they all come back to our relationship with God. "

You see, the questions humans ask reveal more about themselves than they do about God! The heart that says, "How is God loving when....?" reveals something wrong with that person's relationship with God.

Christ's question to the disciples, "Why are you afraid?" was answered by his next statement, "O ye of little faith."

Perhaps Christ did this because of their own question: "Do you not care that we perish?" What kind of a question was that? He was human. He was exhausted from ministry. All they had to do was wake him. He had never failed them yet!

Every problem we have, every bump in the road, every jolt that brings forth what is inside in the form of a question—they all come back to our relationship with God. Church problems, marital problems, job and money problems...all of these issues reveal a basic relationship issue. That is why Jesus said, "Why are you afraid?" Their reaction was directly tied to their relationship with

Him! The disciples doubted Him in this circumstance, and their doubt was exposed by their question.

There is a story of Hudson Taylor seated in an inn with a new missionary in China. He filled a glass with water and then struck the table with his fist. As the water splashed out, he said to the young missionary, "You will be struck by the blows of many sorrows and troubles in China, but remember: they will splash out of you only what is in you."

"There is never a danger of God's being out of control or losing, but there is the real danger of our falling"

Christ's question to the disciples proved to be on target; for when He left them, they evidenced even more fear, asking, "Who is this that even the wind and seas obey His voice?" They truly did not know who Christ was!

Who is Christ? That is a question you and I must answer, from the depths of our heart. Every time. In every circumstance. Who is the God that I am serving? Does He care? Can He keep me?

"Being Martha is not a personality type, but a spiritual disorder."

Paul said in 2 Timothy 1:12, "I also suffer… nevertheless I am not ashamed (or confounded): for I know whom I have believed, and am persuaded that He is able to keep that which I have committed unto Him against that day."

Christ is God, and He is in control even when He appears to be napping!

The disciples cried to Him that they were *perishing,* which meant they felt they were dying, going under, and could not last much longer. We all go through times when we begin to wonder if we can take much more. It looks as if everything is falling apart, for God is sleeping while we are rowing, trying to survive.

Christ could have responded with, "You are not perishing! We are not going down. I am not helpless and out of control in this circumstance."

No matter how bad things get, He is still in control and there is never a danger of His being out of control. The very fact that Christ sent them into the storm was proof He was in control. He knew the storm would come, and He knew what He would do. Christ sends us through places where angels fear to tread and from which humans flee, and He holds us steady through the fiercest storms.

Augustine, the reverend Church Father, spoke of those martyred, whose bodies were ripped to pieces *while their souls remained intact.* What is at danger in any storm is not the body but the confidence, the faith, the spiritual tenacity. Whatever we fear is not nearly as important as our faith in Him!

"There is no mental substitute for His presence."

There is never a danger of God's being out of control or losing, but there is the real danger of our falling into bitterness or some other terrible spirit that eats like a cancer and eventually destroys us. I know of those who have lost their equilibrium, their joy, their poise of soul and their confidence in God in that trying hour; and that loss breaks their relationship with God, filling them with darkness and failure.

A precious family member texted me one time saying, "Disasters and hard times are an opportunity for God to show His greatness and love for us. I wish I had heard this message a few weeks ago. I lost my way."

I responded, "Following God is not easy to do with so many wants inside and uncertainties outside. His still small voice gets lost under all the layers."

She responded, "That's so right. I just couldn't handle the pressure of life and gave up!"

I texted her back, "Perhaps you didn't totally give up. You just reacted as the disciples did in the storm. He has said, 'Peace, be still.' The storm simply reveals the work that God is doing in your life. Don't give up on yourself. He certainly hasn't!"

In John 14:1 Christ says, "Let not your heart be troubled." *Troubled* means to put in motion, to agitate back and forth, to shake to and fro what should remain still, or to cause inner perplexity and emotional agitation by getting too stirred up inside ("upset").

When Christ spoke to Martha, He said her name twice, as if speaking to a child: "Martha, Martha, you are careful and *troubled* about many things" (Luke 10: 41). Being Martha is not a personality type, but a spiritual disorder. Don't live like that! Let not your heart be troubled.

The seemingly sleeping God is still in command. We want to wake Him up, to shake Him, to say, "Do you not see what is going on?" Like the disciples, do we wonder if God knew what He was doing when He sent us across in that boat? Did He know we would face a storm in that direction? God is the greatest meteorologist in our lives. He knows exactly what storms we will face. He might appear to be asleep and out of touch, but He is always more than a match for the occasion!

How do we know that there is a loving God who is in control, that He isn't just some kind of a "3D" image of our reasoning? There is only one answer. Christ proved it when He arose and rebuked the wind. The simple fact that He was there was enough to turn the situation around.

There is no mental substitute for His presence. Philosophy will not rest your mind and heart, but God's presence will.

The Scriptures alone will not do it.

Your past experiences will not do it.

Only His presence brings the rest you so desperately need.

W. J. Harney, a wonderful saint, said, "There is a rest in God, a rest of faith, a rest of mind, a rest of body, a sweet rest, deep rest, abiding rest, undisturbed rest, a rest that brings self-mastery. We are conquerors, yea, more than conquerors, through prayer. If you would live on the mountains of Beulah and be swept by one holy gale after another of God's' perfect love, live much on your knees. If you would be strong in faith and robust in experience, have constant, intimate relationship with God as Daniel did."

The *beginning* of faith is grabbing the rope of His promises, dangling above the dark waters bearing up your ship. The *end* of faith is landing on deck, embraced by the Father, resting in Him. Both ways will get you to port, but what a difference in the trip!

Josh, speaking with me a few days after telling me about his questioning, atheistic friends, said, "I wish they could just be in our services and feel God's presence. Then all would be settled in their hearts and minds."

What an answer! Only God can put to rest our questions and rebuke the winds that threaten to take us down.

Thomas Andrew Dorsey was a black jazz musician from Atlanta. In the 1920s he gained a certain amount of notoriety as a composer of jazz tunes with suggestive lyrics, but he gave all that up in 1926 to concentrate exclusively on gospel music. "Precious Lord, Take My Hand" is one of his best known songs, but there is a story behind this song that deserves to be told. In 1932 the times were hard for Dorsey. Just trying to survive the depression years as a working musician meant tough sledding. On top of that, his music was not accepted by many people. Some said it was much too worldly – "Devil's Music" they called it. Many years later Dorsey could laugh about it. He said, "I got kicked out of some of the best churches in the land." But the real kick came one night in St. Louis when he received a telegram informing him his pregnant wife had died suddenly, along with his newborn. Dorsey was so filled with grief that his faith was shaken to its roots. In the midst of his agony, he wrote the following lyrics:

> Precious Lord, take my hand,
> Lead me on, let me stand.
> I am tired, I am weak, I am worn.
> Through the storm, through the night,
> Lead me on to the light;
> Take my hand, precious Lord, lead me home.

And God will! He knows the path you take, over the rough waters, toward a distant dark shore. He is still in the boat, and He cares enough to lead you home.

Where is your Smile?
finding fulfillment in God's will

When Dan Crawford, a fearless missionary, returned to England after twenty-five years in the heart of Africa, a member of the British Cabinet said to him:

"... modern materialism has robbed the modern young man of his smile."

"I would like to have your eyes. I would like to experience the surprise that you must be feeling when you see the difference between twenty-five years ago and now. What is the biggest change you have noticed?"

His reply? "One of the greatest differences I notice is this: that modern materialism has robbed the modern young man of his smile."

He then referred to the flag that floats over Buckingham Palace. "When the flag floats, the English people know the monarch is in the palace. They smile because they know their beloved ruler is exactly where he or she is supposed to be. The absence of a smile from the faces of the subjects of the King of kings indicates that He does not have the proper place in their hearts."

"They had found death when they least expected it."

It seems the world in our day has also lost its smile. The flag is at half-mast. Men are born missing something, and they ache with the resulting emptiness.

No partner with which to navigate life and its challenges.

No cause for which to live.

No certain destiny.

Is it any wonder their smile is gone?

A young man came one day to William E. Gladstone, the great English statesman and outstanding Christian.

"Mr. Gladstone, I would appreciate your giving me a few minutes in which I could lay before you the plans for my future. I should like to study law."

"Yes," said the great statesman, "and what then?"

"Then, sir, I should like to gain entrance to the bar of England."

"Yes, young man, and what then?"

"Then, sir, I hope to have a place in Parliament, in the House of Lords."

"Yes, young man, and what then?" asked Gladstone.

"Then I hope to do great things for Britain."

"Yes, young man, and what then?"

"Then, sir, I hope to retire and take life easy."

"Yes, young man, and what then?" Gladstone tenaciously asked.

"Well, then, Mr. Gladstone, I suppose I will die."

"Yes, young man, and what then?"

The young man hesitated and said, "I've never thought any farther than that, sir."

Gladstone, looking at the young man sternly and steadily, said, "Young man, you are a fool. Go home and think life through!"

> "We decide there is no good in this world because we are looking at it through the smutted windows of our own souls."

Gladstone had the answer himself and listened intently, and in vain, for it to come from the lips of this young man. The young man had one great vacuum in his life – he had no true purpose.

When men search for a purpose, the great danger of wealth and worldly trinkets appears.

The old English poet, Geoffrey Chaucer, tells us of three happy companions who went out to find and destroy Death.

They met a wise old man and asked him where they could find Death. The old man said: "If you will follow the path through the wood, very soon you will come upon him."

The three young men followed the path, and very soon they came to a great pile of glittering gold. They had met Death, though they knew it not.

This is how it happened:

They agreed that two of them should keep watch over the treasure while the third went to the town to get the means of carrying it away. When the one was gone, the other two began to talk together.

"If we were to make away with the third man, there would be more treasure for each of us."

And while the younger man was in town, the Devil put it into his heart to reflect, *If I were to do away with those two, I should get all the treasure for myself.*

Accordingly, he went into the store and purchased food. He then bought a bottle of wine, put poison in it, and headed back to his "friends."

"Do we really have to drink or "shoot up" or tell ourselves lies in order to prop up a tired smile?"

When they saw him coming, they overmastered him and killed him. Then they sat down to regale themselves on the food that he had brought before they carried away their treasure. After eating, they drank the poisoned wine; and they too fell dead upon the heap of gold.

They had found death when they least expected it.

Such is the discovery of many a man and woman. We find ourselves gazing at the glittering objects dangling from the fingertips of our Enemy.

We are mesmerized by the glaring billboards with their alluring glances.

We are bewitched by the soundtrack of the world singing their songs of love, money, and fame. We want to climb out of the quick-sand of our surroundings and find the solid ground of success that seems to evade so many.

And yet, all we find is one dead end after another, one dashed dream after another. Then we as humans grow tired... tired of trying, tired of looking, tired of dreaming, tired of walking. We drown our sorrows and disappointments with liquor and drugs and cheap relationships. We decide there is no good in this world because we are looking at it through the smutted windows of our own souls.

"His plan to make you happy may not be what you originally envisioned, but it will satisfy beyond any selfish reason or goal. "

When King Solomon had misused his God-given wisdom, squandered his great wealth, and wasted his passions upon women of all nations, he then dipped his pen in the inkwell of bitterness and disillusionment and wrote Ecclesiastes. And the cry that echoes down the halls of that great book is "Vanity, vanity, all is vanity!" or "All is empty and disappointing!"

Tolstoy, in describing what life was to him, told the story of an oriental adventurer who was attacked by a tiger. Fleeing before his foe, the man came to a dry well and instantly leaped into its mouth. The man's hand grasped the stock of a small shrub that grew from the wall of the well and there he held fast. Looking down toward the bottom of the well, the man saw a mad dragon with mouth ajar to snatch and devour him as soon as he fell. With the tiger at the top of the well, and the mad dragon at the bottom, the man determined to hold on to the shrub as long as possible. But just then he saw two mice approach, one black and the other white. They joined labor to begin gnawing at the root of the shrub, and the man could not release his grasp to drive them away.

> "Do we really have to drink or "shoot up" or tell ourselves lies in order to prop up a tired smile?"

There are many besides Tolstoy whose estimate of life is just as discouraging as this picture indicates.

But is this true?! Is that all there is to this old world? Do we really have to drink or "shoot up" or tell ourselves lies in order to prop up a tired smile? Or is there another way?

When Emerson counseled youth, he would say regarding their ambition and aspirations, "Hitch your wagon to a star!"

This is a great saying, but what star? God is the only one making stars to lead people on the proper journey! If we choose to "do our own thing," we will, like so many others, find ourselves disillusioned with life.

Life is very complicated and makes no sense to those seeking their own way. There are too many moving parts, and there is only one Watchmaker who can make your life work like a fine Swiss timepiece!

"The Paintbrush" is a song from my childhood memories. My mother often sang it, and it still plays again and again in my mind. It tells the tale so beautifully:

Life started out like a canvas;
God started painting on me, But I took the
paintbrush from Jesus and painted what I wished to see.

The colors I painted kept running, and the objects
were all out of size. I had made a mess of my painting;
my way now seemed so unwise.

Then I gave my painting to Jesus: all the colors, all the
pieces so wrong. In the markets
of earth it was worthless,
but His blood made my painting belong.

He worked with no condemnation, never mentioned
the mess I had made. Then He dipped His brush
in the rainbow and signed it; the price had been paid.
When I gave the brush back to Jesus, when
I gave the brush
back to Him, He started all over life's canvas to fill,
when I gave to Jesus the brush of my will.

Years ago I had the privilege of pastoring an older
man who had lived the old life of dead ends for years and

then found that there was another answer. He was saved at an elderly age.

I still remember his ten-gallon cowboy hat perched atop a body cut long and lean with a little bit of a curvature to his back around his shoulders, probably due to age. The first time I remember seeing him was right after his conversion. The sight was unforgettable. He was in a camp meeting, expressing his newfound joy and excitement by shouting praise to the Lord and jogging slowly up and down the aisles as best he could. What a sight it was!

"His plan to make you happy may not be what you originally envisioned, but it will satisfy beyond any selfish reason or goal. "

A few years later I had the privilege of pastoring this saint. He was two years from eternity at the time and had been walking with God for a few years. I remember how he would get up and sing a special song for us. Before he started, he would say, "Jesus has a purpose for your life. Find Him, and you will find that purpose!"

And then in his high, tinny voice he would sing from memory "He Touched Me!" I will never forget those days. He had been saved from a life without meaning and an eternity without hope. By the touch of God's hand, he had found purpose in life!

Where is *your* smile?

Remember one thing about God's purpose for your life: His plan to make you happy may not be what you

originally envisioned, but it will satisfy beyond any
selfish reason or goal.

In 1914, just before World War I, a popular French
actress, known on the stage as Eve Lavallier, suddenly
disappeared. She had risen from obscurity to theatrical
prominence and had the world at her feet. Where and
why she disappeared was a mystery to all. At last she was
traced to a small village of the Vosges, where she was
the servant of all needy folk. She spent her days tending
the sick, comforting the sorrowing, bringing joy to little
children, and living a life of prayer and service.

Pressed to return to Paris, she refused. As a girl, she
said, she thought it would be wonderful to be famous.
Having attained her ambition, she was happy for a while.
But the excitement died away and she found herself still
unsatisfied. In service for others she had found what
popularity and applause could never bring, and she was
unwilling to return to life's toys now that she had found
real happiness.

Some years ago, a brilliant young man graduated
from an eastern medical college. He might have become
a prominent city doctor with distinguished patients
and a large yearly income. But on one of his student
vacations, he had taken a journey through the mountains
of Kentucky; and what he saw there he could not forget.
Thousands of people living in the coves and valleys
of that wild region were without any medical attention
whatever. When his classmates inquired where he

expected to practice, he told them that he had pledged
his life to these poor folk of the hills.

In a desolate little hamlet he established his office
and began his career of service. Before very long he
was in constant demand. In any weather, he rode the
mountain trails wherever need called him. The eyes
of the newborn opened on him, as those of the dying
closed on his face in their last glimpse of earth. A pillar
of strength, not only physician but friend, he stood by
all those in trouble anywhere.

After some years an epidemic of influenza found
its way into the mountains. For weeks he gave himself
day and night to its victims, taking no sleep except
what he could snatch on the back of his horse as
he rode from one patient to another. At last, as the
disease waned, he himself contracted it. His strength
reduced by his incessant labors, he could no longer
fight against it.

Almost his last conscious act was to call for his day
book; and across account after account, his weakening
hand scribbled, "Paid in full." Then he died. Stunned
by the death of their good friend, the people assembled
from all directions for his funeral.

Never had there been such a crowd in that
weather-beaten little town. It was as though the whole
countryside had assembled to pay their tribute of
love and respect. They buried him in the bleak little
graveyard on the hillside; then by common consent they

scattered far and wide, each returning with a stone to heap in a cairn on his last resting place.

Then someone had a sudden inspiration. He went to the little store above which the doctor had lived and brought back the sign which hung there. As this sign was placed on the pyramid of stones, the words took on a singular significance—"Dr. Mansfield. Office Upstairs."

> "Have you ever noticed that God never seems to respond to our circumstances the way we do?"

Rude and ignorant as they were, these simple people knew that what their friend had done was a work not even death could stop. The love and skill which he had so freely given them went on with him beyond the grave. He died as he had lived – with a smile on his face.

Are you smiling? Are you happy down deep inside? You should be, if the King is in residence in your heart. May the flag fly high!

Are You REALLY a failure?
Defining spiritual success

D o you feel like a failure? Are you always afraid of your past following you into the future because no matter where you go, you are there?

Perhaps it is a relationship that is not right, a weakness with which you struggle, a habit you have developed that you cannot seem to break.

". . . If people tell you they believe in you, you think, "Yeah, but if they really knew me, would they appreciate me?"

You are definitely not that one who stands in front of the "Gospel Mirror" posing, preening and wondering if everybody else sees how good, how anointed, how spiritual, how above all others you are and deserve to be.

No, you are dragging yourself into church, taking every message from the pastor as a beating from a cat-o'-nine-tails that makes your insides bleed. You have that hangdog look. Sure, you can put on a pretty smile when necessary, but inside it is a different story. You might even wonder if other Christians ever go through what you are facing.

> "...what you think about yourself will ultimately mean the difference between failure and success."

Well, they do!

Martin Luther's wife once came to breakfast dressed in black. He looked up and said, "What's the matter? Who died?"

His wife replied, "Well, dear, I thought that God must have died, the way that you have been moping around the house!"

Like Luther, you may at times be more comfortable alone in a deep, dark dungeon than walking around in the sunshine of God's love and acceptance and freedom.

If you hear a word of encouragement, you think to yourself, "That must be for somebody else."

If people tell you they believe in you, you think, "Yeah, but if they really knew me, would they appreciate me?"

I would like to come to you as a friend, with the backing of God, to talk to you about seeing yourself a little differently; for if you could, it might make a world of difference in how you are living, inside and out.

Someone once said, "Discouragement is one of the most devastating enemies of every good man and of every worthwhile cause. When a man thinks that he cannot succeed, inevitably he does not try hard enough to succeed. There is no greater blight than the expectation of failure." If this fits you, I have something to share.

First, let's see how God thinks about you.

The Psalmist says "When my soul was embittered, when I was pricked in heart, I was brutish and ignorant; I was like a beast toward you.
Nevertheless, I am continually with you; you hold my right hand. You guide me with your counsel, and afterward you will receive me to glory" (Ps. 73:21-24).

"We laugh because we know the truth. Or do we?"

John 14:16-18 says, "And I will pray the Father, and he shall give you another Comforter that he may abide with you forever; I will not leave you comfortless [helpless]: I will come to you."

Does that sound as if He is ready to leave you when you are down? When you don't like yourself? Even when others wag their heads at you?

"He never lost his confidence. He went home a fighter! "

Are you really a failure? To answer this question, I would like to suggest initially that what you think about yourself will ultimately mean the difference between failure and success.

There is an old story about a happy little boy who went out into the field wearing a baseball cap. In one

hand he carried a baseball and in the other a baseball bat.
His face bore a look of tremendous confidence. Cocking
his bat, he tossed the ball into the air, saying, "I'm the
greatest batter in the world!"

Then he swung...and missed.

"Strike one," he said.

He picked up the ball, examined it, and then threw
it into the air again. As he swung, he repeated, "I'm the
greatest batter in the world."

Once again he missed.

"Strike two," he said.

This time, he stopped to examine his bat to make sure
there wasn't a hole in it.

Then he picked up the ball, adjusted his cap, and
tossed the ball into the air for the third time. He repeated
again, "I'm the greatest batter in the world," and swung
with all his might.

"Somewhere along the trail, they quit – on themselves!"

He missed for the third straight time.
"Wow!" he cried. "What a pitcher!
I'm the greatest pitcher in the world!"
We laugh because we know the truth.
Or do we? Perhaps he possessed a greater wisdom than
many of us. You see, he would not be cowed down by his
so-called failures. He never lost his confidence. He went
home a fighter!

I have seen many go home, dragging their bat behind
them spiritually, swearing never to play baseball again!
I have visited many people in their homes who have

not crossed the threshold of a church for many years.
Instead of seeking the arms of a loving church family
and the presence of a loving God, they have purposely
avoided both. Somewhere along the trail, they quit–on
themselves! Perhaps it was something
they heard the preacher say. Perhaps
it was their dad or mom. Perhaps
they looked at others' success and
thought, "I'll never measure up!"

"... don't think about yourself the way you feel about yourself. Instead, go to God!"

A quote attributed to Einstein
says, "If you judge a fish by its ability to climb a tree,
it will live its whole life believing that it is stupid!"

My point is that one of the Devil's oldest tricks
is to beat you down, discourage you, accuse you, and
(most of all) get you to quit! And much of the time, he
does this by using your own opinion of yourself, based
upon a false "measuring stick."

A.W. Tozer, one of my favorite authors, shares
a personal experience along this line:

"It isn't the Lord that has us bound and discouraged.
It is the Devil. One simple act of the Holy Ghost will set
a man free and give him victory. When I was a young
Christian I recall being in an inward jam and the burden
was on me, and I was bound and miserable, walking down
a street in Akron, Ohio.

"Suddenly, I'd had enough of it. I knew God wasn't
mad at me, so suddenly I stopped, and stamped my foot
in the bold daylight, and looked up through the trees

to God, and said, 'God, I won't stand this anymore!' And I didn't. Right there I was a free man!

"Do not accept judgment of your own heart about yourself, *for a discouraged heart will always go astray; so don't think about yourself the way you feel about yourself.* Instead, go to God!"

Elijah was a man of God, but the very same passions with which we struggle also stormed across the mountains and valleys of his soul. God finds him having just run from Jezebel after killing hundreds of false prophets and calling fire down from the heavens upon the sacrifice he had prepared. He had left behind thousands who turned to the Lord because of his stand.

> "Elijah was a man of God, but the very same passions with which we struggle also stormed across the mountains and valleys of his soul."

When the Lord talked to him, he made one request: "Kill me!"

The reason?

"I am a failure!"

God did not share Elijah's opinion of himself and told him so.

Tozer said, "Discouraged Gideon was hiding until God sought him out and said, 'Get up, thou mighty man of valor!' That is certainly *not* how he felt about himself, but he had faith to accept God's judgment of him, and *became* a mighty man of valor!"

Why did God say of Jesus, "This is my Son, in whom I am well pleased"? Certainly, the crowd needed to hear the truth; but so did Jesus. He needed the affirmation of the Father. He needed to know what God thought of Him. And you do, too!

"he had faith to accept God's judgment of him, and became a mighty man of valor!"

It is not enough to think our own thoughts about ourselves. We must hear from God. God's opinion of us often differs greatly from our own, and it is His opinion that makes the difference between continuing the fight and swinging the bat, or going home defeated.

The next question I would like to ask of you who are battling with feelings of failure is this: **"Have you quit?"**

John Bunyan, the famous preacher who spent several years in prison for preaching the gospel in England, wrote a book entitled *Pilgrim's Progress*. In it he depicts the various battles a Christian faces. In one section he describes Christian and Hopeful being caught sleeping on the grounds of Doubting Castle. (Get it?) The giant who lives there is named Despair; and his wife is Diffidence, or lacking confidence. Giant Despair catches Christian and Hopeful early the next

"It is not enough to think our own thoughts about ourselves. We must hear from God."

morning on his grounds and throws them into a dungeon without bread or water, far away from friends and family. It is a sad plight, for Christian is to be blamed for taking the wrong road and landing on Doubting Castle's grounds. That night, Giant Despair asks his wife,

Diffidence, what he ought to do with them. Upon her counsel he berates and beats them. The next morning he tells them they should just end it all because they will never get out. They discuss suicide and decide it is the wrong thing to do. Instead, they take hope that they might be able to get out at some point, for they notice that Despair shakes and becomes weak when the sun shines upon him. (Get it?) The giant returns to see what they have done with themselves, only to find that they are alive and encouraged. He then takes them to the bone yard to see many pilgrims who had come before them and declares that this will be their end by his hand if they do not take their own lives. But back in their cell, Christian remembers a key called Promise that has been hanging around his neck all along. He finds that it fit the locks, and they escape with their lives!

"a young prophet was somewhere in a field, plowing and praying, wishing he could do something better with his life, thinking of how he wanted to be like his hero Elijah."

Please read carefully every innuendo, for Bunyan was trying to portray with every pen stroke the life we as Christians live.

This last year I have been surprised to run into a few Christians holed up in Doubting Castle, under the heavy hand of the Giant Despair! They have been told--and believe--that they are not meant to be Christians. At one time these people were very zealous and devoted to God, but they have lost their way. I want to say, "There is a key around your neck! Use it! Get out of there!"

The word *discourage* means "to tend to stop something or prevent something from happening by making it more difficult or unpleasant; to deter somebody; to stop a person or animal from doing something; to make somebody less optimistic; to make somebody feel less motivated or confident."

The design of Doubting Castle and the Giant Despair is to get you to quit! He can never take your life, but you can!

A personal testimony here. Years ago I was struggling as a young Christian. I was pastoring in Lawton, OK, at the time. My maternal grandfather lived in the same town. Since I had had very little time with him in my growing–up years, I felt it was important to spend some quality time with him when possible. I would go and pick him up in the mornings, and we would drive to a nearby park to walk and visit. Although I did not realize it at the time, those few precious hours were the last ones I would spend with him on this earth. Shortly after we started our visits, he developed cancer and was taken from us quickly. One day, parked in his driveway, I asked him some pointed questions.

"You may not be where you want to be, but are you struggling, listening, and ready to make any change God asks of you?"

"Granddad, you have always seemed to be so steady, so principled, so victorious in your walk with God. What is your secret?"

He then turned to me in his quiet, thoughtful, and courteous way and said, "Mike, what is on the surface is not always what it seems. I'll tell you what I've always told my children. When you fall or stumble, never stay down; get up, say you are sorry, and keep walking. After awhile, you will gain your balance and get stronger and come out on top."

I cannot tell you what his words did for me that day and the rest of my life. I had just heard his secret. He never quit! He was one of the kindest, most conscientious, principled men of God I had ever known. Thank you, Granddad.

"No matter where you are, if you hear the voice of God and are willing to make the change and move, you are headed in the right direction!"

There have been times when I have pulled my own sons aside, sat down on a porch swing, and just talked to them. I have let them know that whatever grace I have found has not delivered me from the struggle. I have told them they will feel like quitting or giving up on themselves, but to keep going. I have shared with them the advice of my grandfather that made such a difference in my life, spiritually.

How many times God has pulled His saints from the mud holes of discouragement, down on themselves!

Elijah asked for death, but God gave him a drink of water and a freshly baked cake. He ate this meal twice and then went in the strength of it forty days and nights! God then showed Elijah the real picture. Seven thousand stood for God. Two kings awaited his anointing for succession. And a young prophet was somewhere in a field, plowing and praying, wishing he could do something better with his life, thinking of how he wanted to be like his hero Elijah.

"Elijah," God told him, "Go anoint Elisha to be your successor!"

By the way, God will never tell you to quit!

"If you have quit trying, get up and go! Not just today, but for always!"

The next question I would ask you if you feel like a failure is, **"Have you stopped changing your ways?"**

A sure sign of the life of God in you is your desire and determination to make the changes that God is asking of you. You may not be where you want to be, but are you struggling, listening, and ready to make any change God asks of you?

"Before you quit and walk away, let me ask you again:"

God is clear: No matter how we feel about ourselves, if we are striving and following, walking in the light as He guides, and making the necessary changes according to His prompting, we are in fellowship and cleansed from all sin! No matter where you are, if you hear the voice of God and are willing to make the change and move, you are headed in the right direction!

The following story is told by a mother:

"My husband and I met each other in church and fell in love. We were married in church; and when our first boy was born we took him with us and put him in the nursery. When he was old enough to walk, he and my husband went hand in hand to Sunday school. As the other children came along, we found it easier just to drop him at Sunday school and go pick him up afterwards.

One Sunday morning at the breakfast table, when he was about seven years old, he was so still and silent that I looked over the Sunday paper to see why. He had stopped eating and was staring into space. His eyes were not focused on anything. I touched my husband with my foot under the table and nodded toward the boy.

"After a moment my husband said, 'Son, what are you thinking so hard about?' His answer jarred us both.

"'Daddy, don't you love Jesus anymore?'

"'Of course, I do. Why do you ask?'

" 'Well, my teacher said that if we loved Jesus we would do what He wanted us to do, and He wants us to come to Sunday school and go to worship services. Daddy, you used to take me to Sunday school and I was so proud of you. Everybody liked you and smiled and shook hands with you and with me, too. I was happy all over.'

"The tears were close to dropping out of his eyes when my husband pushed his chair back and said huskily to the boy, 'Give me five minutes and I'll be ready and we'll walk into that Sunday school together, not just today but for always.'"

If you have quit trying, get up and go! Not just today, but for always!

The last question I would ask of you who think you are a failure is, **"Have you tried to do it all on your own?"** Are you trying in your own strength to be good?

God is clear: We began in the Spirit and we will only be able to finish in the Spirit (Galatians 3:3). Never forget God is your Helper! We have an Advocate!

C. Roy Angell said, "One day I was driving to a luncheon to speak to a group of Baptist preachers. The meeting place was in a part of town that was unfamiliar to me. At one point there was a veritable labyrinth of lanes, streets, and avenues crisscrossing each other. I never got to the luncheon, for some shrubbery obstructed my view and I struck a car that had a right of way. When I finally got home, I called a deacon, Sam Wallace, who is a good attorney and a good friend, and told him that I had a traffic violation and a summons to court. He answered like a real friend.

"'Send me the ticket and I will go in your place.'

"And I said, 'That's just like you, but it isn't that simple. I had a slight accident and did a little damage to another car, so I must go to court.'

"Quickly he answered, 'I will be standing by your side. I will be your advocate.' "The day of the trial came.

Sam and I sat together awaiting the time for me to stand before the Judge. I turned to him.

"'Sam, I'm nervous--this is the first time I ever was on trial. What do I say?' There was sympathy and understanding it his answer:

"'You don't say a word. I'll answer for you.'

"The clerk called my name and we took our places before the bar. The judge turned to my advocate and spoke.

"'How do you plead?'

"'Nolo contendere,' replied Sam. Then he explained what had happened.

"Without a moment's hesitation, the judge said to me, 'I find you guilty.' Then a smile came over his face as he continued, 'But there will be no penalty. Case dismissed.'"

I believe that the Devil has presented his case against me many times and argued that I must be held accountable.

Then God looks at the Son and His sacrifice on the cross, and says, "Yes, he could have done better, but he is forgiven!"

"Since then we have a great high priest who has passed through the heavens, Jesus, the Son of God, let us hold fast our confession. For we do not have a high priest who is unable to sympathize with our weaknesses, but one who in every respect has been tempted as we are, yet without sin. Let us then with confidence draw near to the throne of grace, that we may receive mercy [not justice] and find grace to help in time of need" (Heb 4:14-16).

You have someone on your side: Christ Himself. No matter what you have or have not done, the sacrifice is made and heaven is on your side.

Before you quit and walk away, let me ask you again:

Are you really a failure, or do you need to ask God for His opinion?

Have you quit or are you still struggling, making adjustments?

Have you gone off on your own, trying to be "good" by yourself, or are you leaning upon the everlasting arms of God?

Are you really a failure, or do you just need to say like the little boy with the baseball bat, "Wow, what a great pitcher I am!"?

It *could* make a big difference!

The Tortoise and the Hare
getting to the finish line

There once was a rabbit that ran faster than all the other creatures of the forest. He was rather proud of this fact and mentioned it quite often to the other animals, who grew tired of his bragging.

One day while he and his friends were down by the local watering hole, he grew eloquent on how fast he could run and how nobody could beat him. He suddenly felt inspired to showcase his speed and said, "Let's have a race and see who really is the fastest." Now there was no question

> "The race really belongs not to the swift of foot but to the persistent and enduring, no matter how slow his pace."

that he was the fastest. He simply wanted to show just by *how much* he could beat them. He challenged them all. No takers.

Then one little old stubby-legged creature said in a quiet voice, "I will race you." The rabbit laughed and all the other animals laughed with him. It was a turtle, the slowest of all the creatures of the forest. When all the laughing was done and they had wiped the tears from their eyes, the little turtle said again, "I will race you!" Insulted at first and then indignant, the rabbit agreed to the race just to show the turtle what a fool he was for taking the challenge.

"They have fought the devil and his minions, marching into the wind every step of the way. At the end of their journey all the dark spirits just melted away."

The great day came. They lined up and the gun went off. Down the course the rabbit ran and was quickly out of sight, while the turtle began trudging one stubby leg at a time from the starting line. It was like watching paint dry.

The day wore on and the rabbit was alone, so he decided to take a nap and prove that even with taking a nap he could still beat the turtle. Besides, this race was no fun at all and he was bored.

He awoke sometime that afternoon and heard cheering and shouting. He thought they must be cheering for him; so he arose proudly, stretched himself, and started trotting toward the finish line off in the distance. All of the sudden he saw a little form struggling along in the middle of the path toward the finish line. It was that infernal little stubby-legged turtle! He kicked in the after burners and up flew the dust as he ran. There was still a chance. But long before he even came close, the little turtle crossed the finish line to the cheers of the crowd.

That day the animals learned an important truth: *The race really belongs not to the swift of foot but to the persistent and enduring, no matter how slow his pace.* By the way, the rabbit was never again heard bragging about his speed down at the water hole.

"However, walking looks different in each person's life. We don't all face the same challenges, come from the same backgrounds, and possess the same "wiring" in our personality and character."

James tells us to be a turtle, not a rabbit: "Consider it pure joy, my brothers, when you encounter trials of many kinds, because you know that the testing of your faith develops perseverance. *Allow perseverance to finish its work*, so that you may be mature and complete, not lacking anything….Blessed is the man who perseveres under trial, because when he has stood the test, he will receive the crown of life that God has promised to those who love Him" (James 1: 1-3, 12).

I'm looking for the finish line! I can see the faces of those who have gone on: rejoicing, bearing the scars of victory, welcoming each other. I want to join that crowd. They have fought the devil and his minions, marching into the wind every step of the way. At the end of their journey all the dark spirits just melted away. The journey was done. I remember a saint in my first pastorate who really loved God. She gave liberally and carried souls upon her shoulders. I had not talked to her for awhile and went by her home one day. A stranger answered the door. To my surprise, I learned this saint had gone on. A great solemnity hit me as I realized she had crossed the finish line. When I was a youngster I ran those races at school and remember how I pushed myself, exhausting every ounce of energy I possessed. When I broke the tape at the finish line, I collapsed, relief washing over my body. This godly woman must have felt the same way when she arrived at the end of her earthly race. Like her, I am looking for the finish line!

"Instead, we should understand that God wants to walk with me and you through whatever we have to endure, to teach us and keep us until the end."

To get there we must emphasize walking, not running. (Remember, we are to be a tortoise and not a hare.) However, walking looks different in each person's life. We don't all face the same challenges, come from the same backgrounds, and possess the same "wiring" in our personality and character. The Bible bears this out. We must understand that all stories are different, both the good and the bad. I don't want David's experience of falling with Bathsheba; but on the other hand, I will never slay a giant! I hope I never kill an Egyptian like Moses, but I will also never part the Red

Sea or have my epitaph read "the meekest man who ever lived." I don't want to copy Abraham's example with Hagar, but I will also never be asked to take my son to the mountain to sacrifice him. I don't want to deny Christ as Peter did, but neither will I be one of the stones upon which the church was built and have my name in the foundations of the city of God.

"The stories of these saints include only the highlighted moments, not the grimy, sweaty details of simply living faithfully every day."

What we must realize is that those stories are their stories. Mine and yours are different, unique. We should not compare with others. Instead, we should understand that God wants to walk with me and you through whatever we have to endure, to teach us and keep us until the end. The important part is to see how faithful God was with these saints in every phase of their life.

The next thing is to look more deeply into their stories. The central key to their lives was the fact that they learned how to walk with God. The stories of these saints include only the highlighted moments, not the grimy, sweaty details of simply living faithfully every day. Zacharias was fulfilling his course of duty when he saw Gabriel. Abraham was faithfully following God every day when God would show up every once in a while. Christ said, "Take up your cross *daily*." This means from the top down, thoroughly, in rain and shine. It means that the cross we carry leaves a furrow in the dirt behind us constantly, every day – no

matter where we go, who we are with, or what
we experience.

    I like Enoch. No one ever had to worry about whether
or not he would walk with God any day. The neighbors
didn't have to look out their breakfast window and
wonder if Enoch was going to go on his walk today. He
was known for one thing--walking with God--and he
did it faithfully. The word "walk" means to come and
go, to live. Everywhere Enoch went, God was with him! Then one day, while visiting with God, God made a proposition to him.

"Their faith was like the great current of the Mississippi River, quiet but strong. Flow with it and there is no problem, but try to resist its flow and you find greater power than you ever dreamed."

    "Enoch, I'm going to take you to a different place today. Not on the mountains or down by the creek."

    Enoch perhaps said, "Well, Lord, I don't mind where we go. Everywhere we have been together, I have enjoyed it!"

    So God took him home and he has been up there walking with God ever since. I can see a cowled figure in a boat, somewhat obscured by the misty fog suspended above the waters. He is rowing towards earth's shore. The Lord has told him, "Enoch, there is a saint down there about to cross the finish line. He has walked many a mile and is at the river's edge. Would you go down there and get him?" I see Enoch step out of the boat and take the old saint by the crook of his arm and bear him into the boat. Then I see Enoch begin to row back to the other side of the rivers of death. His boat and the figures disappear into the fog. They land on the shores of sweet deliverance. The walk of this saint is over! The turtle has finished the race.

One challenge we face is to **walk with God steadily, straight through any storm Satan brews up against us and to be found walking the same direction when the dust clears and the smoke is swept away by the wind.**

I'm reminded of those Hebrew boys back in Babylon. I am sure they were the nicest model citizens the courts of Babylon had ever seen. There was something honorable, honest, sharp, and sweet in them. With grace they executed their duties. Their word was gold. People could count on them.

What people did not know was their greatness and model citizenry came from their loyalty to God, which flowed out to the king and his country. Leave that alone and you wouldn't have a problem. Try to put them under your thumb to change their loyalty from God to you and the story was different. You then discovered a solidness and resistance to your hand that you never suspected. From the supper table piled high with the best of food to the prayer closet to the public worship service, these men would not compromise. Their faith was like the great current of the

"They stepped out, and we see them walking the same direction from the fire as when they went in. They just kept walking!"

Mississippi River, quiet but strong. Flow with it and there is no problem, but try to resist its flow and you find greater power than you ever dreamed. Nebuchadnezzar discovered this power in those young men.

I see Nebuchadnezzar's minions spread throughout the countryside, ringing the bells of every dignitary and officer of Babylon. They were to be at the unveiling of the great statue of the king's making. They were all there in their finery with their flashing medals. When the band bore down on the tune they had been practicing, all heads of state hit the ground. All but three, way off in the distance. The king's attention was turned to them. He recognized them, perhaps had patience with them since they came from such different backgrounds and also because they were such good men. He told them they could take five to think about their stand, to reconsider. Their response was immediate.

"There is a life beyond our failures, and it is redeemed by the constant influence of God."

"We can walk out of the darkness of failure and struggles. God is in our future, awaiting our arrival."

"O King, we don't have to take five or sleep on it. We don't have to try to figure out if we will land on our feet or come out smelling like a bouquet of roses. We have already made up our mind."

Their choice to obey and keep walking with God was not based upon the outcomes--it was based upon their commitment to obey God. If you have to reconsider in those times of testing, you have not made up your heart and mind to follow God all the way.

The king's visage was changed toward these boys. He kindled the fire so hot that it would incinerate them instead of just slow-roasting them

"Walking with God is a matter of being faithful, true, and just showing up."

for their impudence! The soldiers threw them in, and a heavenly pocket of air caught their fall. They were walking around in the roar of the furnace, not touched by the inferno. Nebuchadnezzar squinted his eyes, shook his head, and called others to him to witness the scene. Then when the fire had died down a little, he called timidly.

"Shadrach?"

"Yes sir!" the boy answered. The king was shaken but spoke again.

"Meshach?"

"Yes sir!" Meshach smiled back at him.

"Abednego?"

"Yes, O King!"

By this time the anger of the king had subsided and he had lost that authoritative, condescending edge to his voice.

"If you don't mind, come on out here and join us!" the king called once again into the furnace.

They stepped out, and we see them walking the same direction from the fire as when they went in. They just kept walking!

Daniel climbed the same stairs, raised the same window, bent his knees, clasped his hands and raised his eyes toward Jerusalem, praying. When they took him out of the lion's den and set him down, he started walking the same way he went in, toward the heavenly city. He had not changed course!

Another challenge is to **walk in the right direction, after personal failures and disappointments.**

The men who first followed Jesus Christ were not tramps or loafers, but businessmen who left to follow the new preacher. They had found a better reason to live, a higher mission in life. They were now part of the "Jesus Movement." But the day came when they were scattered by Satan's fist and found themselves wondering what to do. Dejectedly, they decided to pick up their old tools and resume the life they had before Christ ever interrupted them. Then Christ suddenly appeared again on the seashore and called out in that familiar voice.

"Children, do you have any meat?"

Jesus had appeared and now called them to recover themselves from their broken faith and past, to follow Him out of the darkness and on into the light!

If we look back through history, we see that David came through the Bathsheba fiasco and walked on back to God and into heaven. Peter recovered from his denial of Christ and became the apostle of lore. Jonah had a ministry after his fish story, and Abraham went on after Hagar and Ishmael to continue his walk with God. We can't go hang ourselves after a failure like Judas did! There is a life beyond our failures, and it is redeemed by the constant influence of God.

We can walk out of the darkness of failure and struggles. God is in our future, awaiting our arrival. Moses had killed a man and lived in remorse for years, but out in the distance a bush was burning and God was waiting to take him on to the next phase of his life. There is a burning bush in our pathway, a fire crackling on the seashore for us as it was for Peter, and Jesus is waiting with open arms.

The last truth I want to share is that we can learn to **walk steadily on through the emotional highs and lows of our relationship with God,** through the storms that brew, unleash their fury, and then pass on through the arch of a distant rainbow. Day after day, we can be found walking steadily, in the same direction.

We do not live in the weather but on solid ground. Our emotions and the storms that blow through our lives are like the clouds that sail across the skies, escorted by the wind--they pass. The awareness of God's presence, the smiles of people, and the blessings of life sometimes come and go like the weather that passes overhead. We can get to the place where we are walking on solid ground instead of checking the weather to determine whether we are "OK" with God or what direction we are going that day. We don't have to dial in to the weather channel to see what life with God will be like and whether or not we are going out to face it. If it rains we put on a slicker and walk. If it snows we put on snow boots and walk. If it is blistering hot we grab our bottle of water and a towel and walk!

One thing God has taught me is to walk with Him with a stride of confidence, trusting Him to make things right, to answer prayer, to meet my needs, and to give me the grace I must have to take the next step. Walking with God is a matter of being faithful, true, and just showing up. Whatever we need is there if we will just keep showing up!

At a local restaurant, I sat by a man who had won the state championship in his past as a body-builder. I asked him about his keys to success in bodybuilding. He then said what he had told so many others: "The hardest part of the journey is parking in front of the gym every morning. That is half the battle. It is all downhill from there."

A world-famous boxer was asked what it took to be a champion. His reply? "Just fight one more round."

James said it like this: "Let patience have her perfect work." Allow time to work its magic! Just keep walking!

One day I looked across the fields where I was walking and talking with God. It was still dark, but I could make out the form of my youngest son Joshua. He was sitting out there on a bench, reading his Bible. The following mornings I witnessed when he would stand at times, looking out across the countryside at the glory of the rising sun. I knew what he was doing. He was learning to walk with God. He was learning to invite God in on a daily basis. This is a walk he will walk the rest of his life, and it will cure all his ills and keep him on track toward the city. Joshua, I will see you at the end of the trail, in heaven some day. Just keep walking!

A grandfather was out walking with his grandson one day. "How far do you think we are from home?" he asked the grandson.

"Grandpa, I don't know."

"Well, where are you?"

"I don't know," the boy said again.

Then the grandfather chuckled and said, "Sounds to me as if you are lost."

The young boy looked up at his grandfather and said, "I can't be lost; I'm with you!" Stay with God!

Like that turtle, we need to keep trudging step by step right past the sleeping rabbit, and before long we will end up at heaven's door and turn back to see how great a distance we covered. At that moment there will be nowhere else to go but in. And Jesus is waiting! Remember, folks, if we keep walking with God, like Enoch, we will end up in heaven!

Be a tortoise and not a hare!